Loneliness of a Small Business Owner
New Revised Edition

Copyright – Stewart Farmer
2014

All rights reserved.

No part of this publication may be reproduced, stored in a retrieval system or transmitted, in any form or by any means, without prior permission in writing of the publisher, nor be otherwise circulated in any form of binding or cover other than that in which it is published and without a similar condition, including this condition being imposed on the subsequent purchaser.

ISBN 978-1-291-73525-3

Business Sorted

www.businesssorted.org

Table of Contents

Chapter 1 – What is a small business?

Chapter 2 – Setting up and running a small business.

Chapter 3 – The essential basics

Chapter 4 – The three lies.

Chapter 5 - Alternative ways to finance your business.

Chapter 6 – Who has their hand in your pocket?

Chapter 7 – HR basics.

Chapter 8 – Compliance

Chapter 9 – Insurance

Chapter 10 – HMRC (Tax and VAT)

Chapter 11 – Small Business Big Problems

Chapter 12 - Collaboration

Chapter 13 – Round up

The Loneliness of a Small Business Owner

About the Author

Stewart has over 30 years of experience working with and helping small businesses in the West of Scotland. He was, until recently, the Regional Development Manager with a UK wide business support Organisation.

This required him to help in the development of Regional policy and to lobby all levels of Government at both local and National up to Scottish Government Ministerial level. He assisted small businesses with problems over a wide range of issues, negotiating and mediating on their behalf, with a range of agencies including local authorities and utility companies.

In recent years Stewart has been part of the Glasgow Economic Partnership, Lanarkshire Economic Partnership and the Ayrshire Economic Forum.

He has a unique insight into how small businesses work and what makes them tick. He understands the pressures and idiosyncrasies involved in running your own business. Stewart has a proven track record in putting forward the case for small business and making the "powers that be" understand what a small business truly is and not the Government view that an SME is less than 250 employees!

He is dedicated to ensuring that Government and other agencies clearly understand the potential of small businesses in growing our economy.

Testimonials

I have known Stewart for about 9 years and in that time, both his knowledge of small business needs and his willingness to offer help and advice has been exceptional.

He has a very good relationship with both local and Scottish Governments along with other business bodies and his contacts have helped with assistance in various aspects of running a small business.
He has always been friendly and efficient with me, in my businesses.

Alan Lyall
Owner and Director
ARL (Scotland)

Stewart was an excellent advocate for the members and committed to serving them to the best of his abilities, often giving up his weekends and spending time away from home to engage with the membership in the more remote parts of his region. He was loyal and trustworthy and the members always spoke highly of him.

Angus Smith
Previous Line Manager

"Just a short note to say how pleased we were with the way you handled our query and the very professional approach you took in advising us.
I have no hesitation in recommending you to any other small businesses who require advice"

J.R. The Flower Basket Stirling

Preface

For more years than I care to remember I have been either running a small business or been involved in helping them in a variety ways.

If you run a small business already you will understand the title of this guide, if you are thinking of or are about to start a business you will soon understand.

Running a business can be a truly enlightening and fulfilling way to earn a living. With careful planning and hard work you too can run your own business. As you approach various agencies for assistance and or finance they will guide you through that maze ensuring you meet your legal requirements and understand cash flow.

This guide is not about the normal help you can get elsewhere. This guide is all about identifying and facing the everyday problems and threats your business will inevitably face. It is how you react to them and what help you seek that will make your business both a success and satisfying as well as being the way you earn your livelihood.

Introduction

The purpose of this guide is to take you past the standard advice you get when you either run or start a new small business.

We will look at a number of issues that impact on the day to day running. Not always things that you have expected and more importantly are more common that you would imagine.

In Chapter One we take you through exactly what constitutes a small business and how they fit into the larger economic picture and their local community.

Chapter Two Is designed to give you a rough idea of what attributes are best for running a small business and the various problems you may have fitting it round your family life.

Chapter Three looks at the basic essentials such as business plans, opening a business bank account, assessing what grants and assistance may be available, looking at possible premises etc.

With Chapter Four we look at your interaction with the various agencies that you will have to interact with throughout your business life. There are some important pointers on how to maintain a good relationship with them.

How do you finance your enterprise? In Chapter Five we examine a range of alternative ways to finance your business other than the normal sources such as banks.

In Chapter Six we examine the numerous and varied scams aimed at businesses. We name the most common and how best to ensure you are not caught out.

Small Businesses are an often overlooked source of new jobs. Legislation and a lack of HR knowledge contribute to this. Chapter Seven is all about the dynamics of employing in a small business. It is not an HR guide as such. It will alert you to how employing can impact on your business and why current legislation can overly impact on the smaller company.

Compliance is a huge problem for small businesses with laws being made to suit larger companies and their resources. Chapter Eight looks at how small businesses have to adapt to meet the regulations.

Do I need insurance and if so what do I need? Chapter Nine will look at the basics.

Tax and VAT can be problematical for any company never mind a preoccupied and busy small business owner we tackle some of the basics in Chapter Ten.

Chapter Eleven looks at the variety of unforeseen problems that can spring up at any time causing disruption and a lack of focus.

In Chapter Twelve we look at collaboration with other small businesses in order to broaden your range of services.

Finally in Chapter Thirteen we round up the main points

Chapter 1

What is a small business?

Government terms a small business or SME as they like to refer to them as a business of less than 250 employees. However, in Scotland, 98% of businesses employ less than 50 people with over 90% employing less than 10.

Often in discussion I am told by business owners that they are "really small" and I get the impression they don't truly believe they are a "real business". As you can see from the figures they are by far and away the most common type of business in the country.

Every small business makes its own contribution to the overall economy and to the local economy of which they are an integral part. They supply jobs to local people and, more importantly they keep money in the community. If you think of small businesses as a "Sector" they form a powerful grouping making them powerful contributors to the economy at all levels.

A small business has the ability to be much more nimble than a large one, they can diversify more quickly and adapt to changing markets and more recently economic conditions.

A small company is more likely to make a greater effort to retain staff in a recession. Once they have found the right employee and invested in them by way of training they are aware of losing that skill and having to start again when the upturn comes makes little sense.

It may mean shorter hours, job sharing or a wages cut but they will try harder to retain a valued employee.

Small businesses come in many forms be it self-employed, partnerships, a few employees, a limited company or a family business that has been passed down, each one as individual as its owner. There are no special rules governing what makes a small business owner.

They need a good idea, clear planning, a determination and belief to succeed.

Some owners have a vision of growing their business. While others are what I would call "lifestyle" by which I mean the owners are running a business that is bringing in sufficient earnings to fund the lifestyle they are happy with. Bed and Breakfasts and holiday lets are often good examples.

It is important to understand that not all small businesses are the same no matter your size and aspirations every business is important, in its own way, to the economy.

There is a lack of understanding by Government and some agencies that have a tendency to try and enforce a one size fits all set of solutions and incentives when offering advice, training and finance initiatives. The finance initiatives in particular are usually not suitable for the vast majority of businesses. Why is this the case? Remember the 250 employees or less?

People start a small business for numerous reasons. The owner has been made redundant or currently unemployed and believes that by working for themselves they can make a living. If you have a skill and the appropriate contacts you can succeed.

Many people start a small business as a lifestyle choice. This type of business tends to be much more likely in rural and tourist areas.

They will mostly recruit from the local area supplying much needed jobs. They are valuable sources of employment in their community and deserve the same support as other small businesses.

They have difficulty with HR issues, complying with Health and Safety and dealing with tax and vat because they do not have specialist knowledge and have to, in many cases, buy this expertise in. I believe this weakness is what discourages many businesses from expanding, hence my earlier remarks about targeted assistance.

This is often much more important than finance which tends to dominate Government thinking.

Having established what a small business is and some basic principles should you do it? Yes! If you believe you have a good idea, a niche market to aim for or even a different take on an old idea. If you are prepared to put in the hours and virtually live the business go for it.

This guide will help to take you through the maze of likely and often unexpected pitfalls and problems that you may encounter on your journey to success.

When the Government tells us that small businesses are the bedrock of our future growth I believe they truly mean just that. Unfortunately they have no real understanding of what a small business really is. Why do I believe this? You only have to look at the reams of legislation that is produced, most of it is designed for larger companies with their own separate departments and resources to deal with things like, Employment Law and Health and Safety. In a small business you are that and every other department.

There is a failure to understand that some of the legislation impacts unfairly on a small business. A good example is paternity leave. In a large company a couple of people taking paternity leave can be mitigated for quite easily. In a three or four employee company one person means 25% of your workforce has gone.

They are also, currently, the most underrated source of new jobs. With a little targeted help there are opportunities for many more jobs to be created.

Chapter 2

Setting up and running a small business.

What attributes do you need to run a small business? You should have confidence, enthusiasm and a belief in your business idea. You will need to be prepared to work long and often unsocial hours and be available for your customers 24 hours a day 7 days a week if that is what they want. Your family, at least in the early days, will probably have to come second.

It is important that your family fully support your decision and understand what is likely to be involved.

In the beginning you may experience friction and competing demands on your time. This will be particularly true if you work from home. Often because you are always around the family may think that this means you are available.

At the start lay down ground rules, even setting aside certain times where you will be at work and as such unavailable.

For instance a big non - starter is family members trying to interrupt you while you are on the phone, this can't happen. Nothing sounds more unprofessional than if you are in the middle of an important conversation with a supplier, a client, your bank, than you having to break off and point out to some-one you are on the phone.

If you decide to work from home try to set aside a room or in an ideal world set up a garden office to run the business from. This allows a physical separation of the business from family life.

If you can possibly manage it, keep the business separate from the family life. Don't have files stacked up on the coffee table or tucked into the kitchen cupboards.

There will be times when business and family clash. If you have agreed a set of rules at the outset don't backslide. When the inevitable occurs explain that business comes first, this will be particularly true when you are starting up.

Check your house insurance. Will it cover your business equipment? Are there any local by-laws that might impinge on running a business from home? It is also worth checking planning regulations if you are storing goods, equipment or vehicles. It can be a good idea to let your direct neighbours aware of your plans and get them onside.

Will you use your or the family car for business purposes? If so ensure you check your current insurance will cover you. It will be well worth the extra few pounds on your premium to guard against accidents.

How do you deal with business mileage? HMRC requires you to keep a note of all business mileage. Note the start of the journey and the end. You are entitled to claim business mileage at the rate of 45p per mile for the initial 10,000 miles then 25p per mile thereafter.

The business could also purchase the vehicle however the tax implications can be onerous. You would be taxed as a benefit in kind. For instance if you buy a £25,000 car you will pay tax on whatever rate you normally do on 26% of this figure which equates to at the 20% rate £1300 or £2600 if you are a higher rate tax payer at 40%

Keep a note for when you have to complete the annual tax return. Keep a notebook in the vehicle and note starting mileage and finishing mileage. This also gives you a record for the tax man should he require proof.

To recap:

You will need to be enthusiastic and committed.

Try to keep family and business separate. If this is not possible set the rules of engagement and make sure everyone understands.

Unless your idea requires it, switch off your phone and resist the temptation to check your emails, you would be amazed how often you pop into the office for five minutes after dinner and find yourself there a few hours later. Not a recipe for a happy family life.

Starting a small business? What is the best set up for you?

This is a key question when setting up and it is important that you appreciate the pros and cons of each type of set up.

Starting up your own small business can be a daunting decision, but, do it correctly and it could turn out to be a great decision. Now is a good time to start a business. A downturn should be seen as a test, succeed when things are tough and it follows that you can go on to become even stronger.

However, your chances of success depend on making a number of important decisions, one of which is business structure will suit what you plan to do

There are three common business structures for startups. Each has its own advantages and disadvantages and should be carefully considered, as the profitability and success of your business can hinge on the choice that you make.

Sole trader

This is the simplest setup. You won't need to register with Companies House. As a sole trader, effectively you are the business and can take on employees like any business. The "sole trader" refers to you being the sole owner of the company not that you work alone. You keep all the profits of the business after tax. However you are also personally responsible for any debts or liabilities and losses that may be made. Other responsibilities include completing a self - assessment tax form each year, paying on profits and pay national insurance.

You will also have legal responsibility for your business and its actions (which can leave you exposed to much greater risk than other structures including possible actions against you as an individual), so a comprehensive insurance policy should be a priority.

Partnership

Partnerships are often similar to a sole trader set-up – only they have more than one owner, and each are jointly and personally responsible for the business's entire debt, if one partner walks out, for example. A limited liability partnership (LLP) is a more protective for individual partners as it limits liability to what each partner has invested in the business.

You do have to register with Companies House and put certain information on the public record if you decide to go down third route, much like a limited company.

Sole traders and partnerships can also benefit from savings on tax when it comes to providing benefits in kind. For example, providing yourself with a car for business travel can be far more tax efficient than through a limited company structure.

Limited company

Limited companies are a different proposition altogether. Companies must be registered with Companies House and pay 20% corporation tax on profits.

Payroll taxes (under PAYE) are also a consideration, although this is the case where you have employees in any setup.
You basically have a choice of whether to pay yourself a salary or dividends, with this option, but it is advisable to pay a salary of at least a modest amount, if only to keep your entitlement to state benefits. The company can also lend a director money. To be clear on how this would affect you check on www.hmrc.co.uk

Dividends can offer business owners a very competitive tax rate compared with salaries, but on the other hand, they don't qualify for pension relief, and are not a tax-efficient method of growing your retirement pot.

Chapter 3

The Essential Basics

A Business Plan

Most start-up businesses are somewhat afraid of the idea of preparing a business plan. However, it is not especially difficult process, the best business plans help you focus on your goals as well as assisting in securing finance and support.

The business plan will help to crystalise your business idea and define your long-term objectives. It provides the basis for running the business and a way of checking your progress. It is also vital for getting finance from whatever source.

We will explain:

1. What needs to be included?
2. Showing your financial forecasts.

Summary

We will show you how to outline your business proposal. Usually this is the last part to be written, it will be the first page of the business plan. Keep it clear and concise bearing in mind most people reading it will not be experts in your business. You need to get the main points over without any jargon.

Main Points

- What are you offering in the way of services or products?

- What is your target market and probable competition?
- Your previous experience.
- Financial projections including draft cash flow.
- Sources of funding and any conditions attached.

When making a decision about supporting a start-up, bank managers and investors will likely make an initial decision based on your executive summary so it is important to get the basics across at this point, with key pointers to the relevant back up information.

- They will then read the detailed plan to back - up their initial decision. An appendices should carry detailed information to support the main assertions in the summary.

Explain your business idea, including:

- How long you have been developing the business idea in its present form.
- What work and research you have done so far.
- All related experience you have.
- The intended structure of the business. (see Chapter 2)

Explain clearly what your service or product is.

- How it differentiates from other products or services
- The customer base you expect to be buying your product or service

- Your plans to develop the business as it grows and your customer base grows and their demands alter.

- Be clear about any weaknesses and how you intend to tackle them, remember about being honest. It shows you are aware of what difficulties there may be and that you have planned to deal with them.

Define your marketplace and any particular segments you intend to concentrate on and why.

- Show the size of each market segment and if it is growing or contracting.
- If possible, show the trends in the marketplace.
- What research have you done to ensure your product will work in this particular market?
- If you have already lined up any sales you have ensure you mention them and if you have closed any deals.

Who are your competitors and how are you different

- Make a list of the advantages and disadvantages of your main competitors and their products.
- Explain why you believe people will switch to your competing product.
- It is important that you understand your competitor's products or services and how you intend to counter them

- A strong market is essential and you must be able to clearly demonstrate that you will be able to compete.

You must show you have done the market research needed to justify what you say in the plan.

Selling and marketing your business

This section is vital, often gives illustrates the business' chances of success.

Is your product or service tailored to meet your customers' needs?

How do you see the positioning your product?

> You should show how your price, quality, response time and after-sales service will compare with your competitors.

How do you intend to sell to customers?

For instance, what will be your principal method of selling, face to face, online, word of mouth etc.?

- Give an indication of long you expect each individual sale to take.
- Will you be able to make repeat sales? If not, growth may be difficult.

Who will be your initial customers?

- Do have a list of potential customers who have expressed an interest or promised to buy from you and the quantity of sales they represent.
- How will you identify potential customers?

You should be able to show you have a potential customer base.

What are your plans for advertising the service or product? Will you use internet, social media, events or print advertising?

If more than one product or service is being offered to what extent will each contribute to the profitability of the overall business?

- Most businesses need more than one product, and a fairly wide variety of customers
- Closely examine each item and look at cost of sales and margins.
- Identify where you may be able to increase the profit margin

Services can be more difficult to market. Start-ups in these areas must pay special attention to marketing.

Management

People reading the business plan need a concise understanding of how the business will be managed and the quality and experience of the management team.

Show the strengths and weaknesses of the team.

- Define each management role and who will fill it.
- Show your strengths and indicate how you will tackle any weaknesses.
- Show the background and experience of each team member.
- What systems will you put in place to keep control of the business?
- Show what help and support, including mentors you have.

Are you committed?

- Banks and any other potential investors will want to be sure you are committed to the business. Show how much time and money each of the management team will contribute.

What are the facilities you will need to start up? Some small start-up businesses only need a desk and a phone.

- Consider any potential limits to production capacity or ability to provide services.

If you are going to manufacture or distribute products, show how and where you are going to warehouse them and for how long.

Sales forecasts produced for start-up businesses are almost always over-optimistic. Here are the reality checks.

How soon can you start selling?

- Are potential customers prepared to start ordering in sufficient amounts from the start or will there be a delay?

How much time can you dedicate to selling?

- How many days can you sell?
- How long will it take to establish credible leads?
- What is the forecast percentage of leads that will turn into sales?

How soon after a sale can you collect payment?

What will, realistically, be your sales income each month?

Financial forecasts (Draft Profit and Loss, Balance Sheet and Cash Flow Forecasts)

This translates your business plan into numbers.

A realistic sales forecast is the basis for all your other forecasts.

- Break the total sales figure down and show the contribution of each to the total sales figure.

Your cash-flow forecast does exactly what it says. It shows how much money will go through the company and highlight any week spots.

- Show when there will be more money coming in than going out ('cash-positive'). Also be honest about when there may be negative cash flow and what you have in place to counteract this.

Your profit and loss (P&L) forecast shows how the business will be moving forward. Show the annual P&L forecast for each of the first two or three years of trading.

Balance sheets are often not required for very small startups but should be included where possible.

These will show the projected financial state of your business on day one and at the end of the trading period, perhaps for the first two or three years.

Your forecasts are not infallible. You may need to revise them.

For your forecast, make a list all your key assumptions (e.g. prices, sales volume, and timing). Small business advisers at banks and your local business support organisation will often help you put together your forecasts free of charge.

Financial requirements

The cash-flow forecast will show how much finance the business needs and when it will be required, your assessment of the figures will decide whether or not you need to arrange alternative funding.

Explain how much finance you will need, and in where you expect to access it.

For example, you might want a fixed-interest loan and an overdraft facility. Or you can examine the many alternatives.

Show how you intend to use the finance?

- You should be able to show how any finance would be used for buying equipment and how much for working capital (financing stock and debtors).

Show how you intend to gain finance and how you will pay for it.

Show you understand and have assessed the risks

Show in the business plan how you would deal with any setbacks such as a main customer failing.

- Explain what you would do if it actually happens?

You should include a detailed Cash-flow, Draft Profit and Loss and if applicable Draft Balance Sheets for at least two years.

Show back up information

- A detailed CV and general back ground of the key personnel involved (you will need this if you are looking at outside funding).
- Show what market research you have done.
- Any marketing literature and, if appropriate any technical specifications.
- Who are you main customers going to be

Presenting the plan

The better the quality of the information you have, the better the business plan will be. Remember that a concise Executive Summary is essential as most people reading the plan will not have time to read the detail in the first instance so you must get their interest to encourage them to delve deeper.

Keep it Simple Stupid (KISS)

- Keep it short sharp and to the point illustrate your intentions and aims without flowery addition.

Make sure it looks professional.

- Put a cover on the business plan and give it a title.
- Include a contents list.

Check it, check it and check it again then get someone else to read it through.

- Re-read it yourself. Does your plan give anyone reading it a clear idea of what your business is about?
- Let friends and any professional contacts read it, does it make sense to them?

Start – Up Assistance

Most local authorities have their own internal Economic Development department. This will cover items and support such as start - up loans and grants, employment initiatives and targeted funding usually aimed at employing particular sectors from the unemployed. Currently employing young people is a key policy. Depending on the local council the level of influence in the marketplace will vary. For assistance Glasgow City now has Jobs and Business Glasgow which is seen as the umbrella for all employment issues within the city boundaries.

Following on from this we have a Scottish wide Business Gateway service which delivers help, advice, support and training mainly to start – up businesses. Some of the Gateways are run under external contracts and others are run by the local council area that they are responsible for. In either case you should get the same level of service and the same services across the board.

Business Gateway can, in the early days, offer valuable insight and support especially when you are deciding on forms of finance, bank accounts and how to market your business. They do not offer finance themselves but can direct you to various schemes that are available in their area. As already suggested these are likely to be local council initiatives. There are in some areas loan funds which will offer 50% matched funding. There is the East of Scotland Loan Fund and the West of Scotland Loan Fund for instance. There may be not for profit loan schemes such as DSL Finance for Business they will introduce you to.

The Gateways also have a vast amount of company information which you can access with regard to marketing and credit worthiness of possible customers. Training in various aspects of business disciplines are an important element in the Gateway offering. They will offer training in the basics such as accounts, tax (self - assessment and PAYE), VAT, employment issues, health and safety, basic computing courses and social media training across most of the popular platforms such as twitter, face book and linked in.

Useful Agencies

Business Gateway

Business Gateway is a Government led agency with the remit to help and assist small business. It is important, from the outset to understand that they do not supply funding or grants. However they have information on many of the national and local incentives that are in place and should be able to put you in touch with the mainstream finance sources.

They will give assistance in the following areas

Starting up a business

Business support and advice

Form a company or business

Naming a business

Buy a business or franchise

Create business plan

Intellectual property

How I turned an idea into a successful business - case study

Make your brilliant idea a reality

Business Plan Template

Growing Your Business

Business support and advice

Form a company or business

Naming a business

Buy a business or franchise

Create business plan

Intellectual property

How I turned an idea into a successful business - case study

Make your brilliant idea a reality

Business Plan Template

Benchmark business performance

New ideas

Suppliers and outsourcing

Joint ventures and business partnering

Financing Options

Funding and financing

Grants and benefits

Accounting, financial management

Cash-flow, invoicing, payment management

Tax returns

Tax rates and allowances

Insurance

Sales & Marketing

Marketing

Exporting, importing

Website design, management, optimisation

Your Local Authority Economic Development Team

In some respects this will mirror some of the Business Gateway offerings, in fact, some gateways are run by the local council. The principal difference is that the Economic Development departments will deliver the local initiatives such as start – up loans and grants along with employment incentives. Examples include incentives to employ youngsters and long term unemployed or Graduate Placement Schemes.

In terms of localised finance, each local authority will have particular schemes that are peculiar to them.

Skills Development Scotland (SDS)

SDS is a national body created to deliver a consistent skills agenda across all sectors.

Adopt an Apprentice

The Big Plus

Career Management Skills

Certificate of Work Readiness

Employability Fund

Employer Recruitment Incentive

Energy Skills Challenge Fund

Flexible Training Opportunities

Individual Learning Accounts

Low Carbon Skills Fund

Modern Apprenticeships

Our Skills - force

My World of Work

PACE Redundancy Support

Provider Central

Remploy Employment Incentive

Business Scotland

www,business.scotland.gov.uk

This covers a variety of topics

Recruitment

New ideas and innovation

Waste reduction and management

Energy efficiency

Business tax

Intellectual property

Funding and grants

Starting up a business

Research and development (R&D)

Events, conferences, trade shows

Health and safety

Market research

File company information with Companies House

Contracts and tenders

Licences and permits

Environmental responsibilities

Carbon reduction

Benchmark business performance

Regulations

Productivity and performance

Networking

Marketing

Information Technology

Register a new company or partnership

Check company details with Companies House

Business rates

Business planning

Website management and social media

Value Added Tax (VAT)

Pollution and prevention

Planning and building control

Bankruptcy and insolvency

Managing people

Joint ventures and business partnering

High growth business support

Doing business in Europe

Dismissing staff and redundancies

Workers' rights and discrimination

Data protection

Chapter 4

The three lies.

They say there are three great lies in the world:

1. The cheque is in the post
2. Of course I will still love you in the morning
3. I am from the Government and I'm here to help you!

As you will learn from my later chapter on scams you will see, hear and read a lot of untruths and statements that are devious and false. However you will learn to see through these with experience and that correct advice.

Always try to be honest in your dealings with suppliers and customers. However there are three people this is imperative for when running your business.

First your bank manager. For most of us they are our main source of funding and as such have a great deal of power and influence on the success of your venture.

Always be proactive with the bank. If you know that you are going to come up short on funds coming in, tell them.

Banks hate surprises. If you know that paying this week's wages may be a problem tell them. If payments coming in are slow or are late, tell them. Get into this habit and do not stick your head in the sand and hope it will all be alright, it won't!

If you build up this kind of relationship you will find that, in most cases, the bank will be much more flexible with you. For example if you are short for the staff pay that week or month but can show you have money due in the next few days, if you have built up a solid relationship showing that you are reliable, they will be much more likely to help you.

Secondly with HMRC, both VAT and Income Tax. Avoid being found out and pay the penalty. Always, always keep your PAYE and VAT payments up to date. By doing this you are less likely to be flagged for any sort of enquiry.

HMRC have a job to do, accept that. The horror stories of how they hound small businesses out of existence are untrue if you are honest and fair with them, they will be honest and fair in return.

HMRC are very approachable. If you have questions contact them and get the answer.

They also run courses for PAYE and VAT at no cost to teach you what they expect of you and how the various forms required to be filled in. Go to http://www.hmrc.gov.uk/ to find your nearest office and give them a ring.

Many people are afraid to contact the "tax man" in case they draw attention to themselves. Don't be, you are much more likely to draw attention to yourself with late or incorrect payments.

Finally, and perhaps most importantly, you have to be honest with yourself. It can be all to easy to kid yourself on that everything is really OK and the next order is just around the corner and it will all work out.

Working for yourself is lonely, and it is all too easy to find yourself in bubble slightly detached. You can easily become inward thinking and because you're the boss and the buck stops with you and you can't always trust your own judgement.

What I mean by this is, that plan in your head may seem a brilliant idea but can have flaws that you do not see because you are too close and often too eager for it to succeed.

Who do I ask? Initially you can ask your partner or member of the family as long as they are not part of the business.

This will have drawbacks, not least your family may be tempted not to hurt your feelings and may hold back from the very criticism you require. Ideally you need someone who is emotionally remote from you.

A good start would be a business advisor through Business Gateway or a mentor. If you started your business through the Princes Trust you will have a mentor assigned to you. In Scotland you also have Business Mentoring Scotland and The Scottish Mentoring Network.

They can be contacted at www.businessmentoringscotland.co.uk or www.scottishbusinessnetwork.co.uk

Another alternative is to employ a mentor/trouble-shooter depending on exactly what you need. This type of service is useful when setting up, just discussing the initial idea and forward plans with an objective person can be crucial. You are perhaps struggling and require advice and a little third party expertise to give you an objective perspective. This can be excellent value for a small outlay.

My own business offers this service at either an hourly rate or short fixed term contract.

Our service includes basic mentoring, objective analysis and access to a wide range of contacts. Check our web site www.businesssorted.org

Chapter 5

Alternative Ways to Finance your Business

In a recent and important development banks who are unable to supply finance to client businesses have a requirement to assist them by signposting other forms of available finance from a variety of sources.

There is now a service called "Alternative Business Funding" (ABF) they supply through their website, and I quote:

"alternativebusinessfunding.co.uk is designed to provide free and easy access selecting alternative business funding for SME's – especially those with an interest in alternatives to traditional bank loans or asset finance. Our traffic light interface will guide you to the most appropriate funder after answering just a few quick questions about your business. All the funders on the site are the market leaders in their sector"

These include Pension Led Funding, Funding Circle, Zopla, Angels Den and Crowd Cube. The various funders are being added to on a regular basis.

Why do we need Alternative Finance?

I have, in the past, run a number of events for small businesses to give them the opportunity to investigate the alternatives to traditional bank funding. With official figures pointing to around 56% of Scottish businesses looking for funding then a look at other ways of achieving finance is very important.

For most businesses there are traditional sources of finance, the banks being the most likely. You will be acutely aware that in the past few years bank lending to small businesses in particular has become difficult.

This is despite many unsuccessful attempts by Government to rectify the situation by tempting the banks with various schemes. The problem encapsulates the deep misunderstanding of the type of funding that is required by small businesses. Many of the initiatives are aimed at the higher range of borrowing. A good example is the Scottish Development Bank set up to develop private sector funding to the small business market. Unfortunately it has a minimum borrowing requirement of £250,000. This is not where the funding gap exists. The problem for the hundreds of thousands of micro businesses that they only require relatively small amounts of funding. Whether it be to upgrade machinery, buy a van or diversify.

These businesses are looking for amounts below £20,000 generally. So you can see we have a huge credibility gap.

This chapter will give you some ideas of how to raise that funding.

Family and Friends

In some circumstances this can be a good source of finance but only if the lenders are clear about the possible downsides. If you go down this route it is best that you put a formal agreement in place and treat it as you would any other kind of loan. The amount borrowed, the interest rate and how and when it will be paid back.

It may be a family member may be willing to invest in return for a share of the business again a clear agreement must be put in place.

Start - up Loans

There are a number of basic start-up loans available. Many Local Authorities will have a small fund to assist start-ups. This may be as a loan or a grant.

The Princes Trust will provide start - up funding provided that you are under the age of thirty.

They will also make available loans and development loans at very reasonable rates.

You can get full information from http://www.princes-trust.org.uk/

Grant Funding

This is a much more cluttered landscape with different local authorities having differing priorities and as such offering varying grants. It can often be a post code lottery as to whether you are eligible or not. Again the Princes Trust will offer small development grants of up to £500.

Many grants are reliant on a number of factors such age or location or type of businesses. There are a large number of obscure grants out there which go back to the days when coal mines and steelworks were closed and funding was put in place to assist. Many of these are still live. A great place to find out what is available in your area and business type is http://www.j4b.co.uk/ this will lead you through the maze of what is available.

Loan Funds

Loan funds are most often available only as matched funding in other words as 50% of any other funding you may have access to. In Scotland there are two excellent examples. There is the West of Scotland Loan Fund http://www.wslf.co.uk/ and the East of Scotland Investment Fund http://www.eastscotinvest.co.uk/

Another great source of loan funds are through sector specific schemes such as environmental and green projects. Also there is funding available for training and skills improvement.

Not for Profit Lenders

A great example of this type of lender is DSL Business Finance. DSL offer loans from £1,000 to £50,000 over a period of 2 to 5 years. The fact that they are non - profit making means that money they do make is recycled back into the business.

The only slight drawback is that often this type of lender will be a little more expensive because the risk is often greater.

DSL also operate the Enterprise Finance Guarantee which allows businesses to "buy" access to funding when they have insufficient security to do so. This is a common problem for start - ups.

You are 100% responsible for the debt, however there is a government guarantee in place which provides the lender with security. DSL can offer up to £30,000 under this scheme. Check it out at www.dsl-businessfinance.co.uk

Enterprise Loan Guarantee

As already referred to this is a government based scheme to offer security to lenders for business loans they make in order to kick start the market. Through the scheme you can borrow up to £1 million.

Lending decisions are made on the basis of the ability of the borrower to service the debt. The level of personal financial commitment that you have in the business will also be a factor.

With EFG other forms of security can be used in addition to the scheme, personal guarantees for instance, but not any form of security based on your home.

There is a 2% premium on your annual reducing balance which you would pay quarterly.

You can find more details on the EFG scheme at https://www.gov.uk/understanding-the-enterprise-finance-guarantee

Floating Charge

A floating charge is similar to a fixed charge. A fixed charge is when you borrow money to buy something like a building, a car or machinery. You will not be able to sell this asset without the lenders permission as they would have first call or charge on the item if you were unable to pay the debt. Think mortgage and you are pretty much there. A floating charge is usually taken by someone like a bank where they have first call on your outstanding debtors.

Invoice Factoring

It used to be that invoice factoring was not available to small companies as their turnover was considered to be too low to make it viable.

This is not the case now with factoring being available across the board. What is factoring and how does it work?

The finance company or bank you approach will check your credit record and those of your prime customers and if you wish to add or take on new customers you will require approval from the factor to have them included.

This does not mean you cannot take on new clients or customers, however if the factor believes they are a risk and will not take them on board you will have to invoice them separately and deal with them directly.
In its simplest form you do the work for a client or sell a product then you raise the invoice.

You then submit that invoice to your bank or finance company.

The invoices are then checked and verified, so as to ensure that rogue invoices are not being raised to create extra funds.

You will then receive between 80 and 85% of the invoice value by return.

The factor will then credit control the invoices, this can be a real boon to a small company who does not have the resources to have a dedicated credit control person.

When the invoice is paid you will then receive the balance less the agreed costs.

Some companies will seek personal guarantees from the business owner, this is a decision for you to make. It means that you are, in effect, underwriting any unpaid invoices. Think carefully before you commit to this if asked.

Selective Invoice Finance

Works in the same vein as normal invoice factoring. The major difference being that you can be selective. The only restriction is that you must me a limited company to benefit from this form of financing.

Single Debtor deals mean that you can choose just one particular debtor from you customers that you wish to factor. This may be because of the high proportion of business they generate or it may be they are always high value invoices. This applies also to which invoices you decide to put forward for factoring. Most traditional factors will be expecting to factor the majority if not all of your debtor book.

It can be used to fund export invoices staged invoices and even confirmed forward orders. This can expedite a variety of business entities including new starts. The agreed fee will include an insurance premium to ensure credit protection is in place. The debt must be verifiable and credit insurance must be available.

One such source of funding are Working Capital Partners and this is how they explain the service they offer.

"Whether you have just started up your business or you are ready to expand, Working Capital Partners provides a cash flow solution that can really help your business grow.

Working Capital Partners offers unique [selective invoice financing services](#) that allows you to sell selected invoices to raise immediate cash. Some factoring companies insist that all invoices are discounted but at Working Capital Partners we believe in offering [complete flexibility to our clients](#) who choose which invoices to discount as and when needed.

Unlike other factoring companies, we do not collect payment from your suppliers – we leave this to you so that your relationships with your own suppliers remain intact. As long you are a limited company, have a genuine invoice and your customer is creditworthy, we can make an advance of up to 85% of an invoice, often on the same day. At Working Capital Partners, there are no on-going administration fees or funding charges, just a simple fee for each invoice sold."

What makes this form of finance different?

- Fast decisions
- Is flexible
- Client retains credit control
- Simple flat fee
- Has no hidden charges
- No minimum charges or ongoing commitment
- Client can "walk" away at anytime

Where this system is helpful is: Seasonal Businesses such as florists card retailers.

'Top' up existing Bank Overdraft where the facility is either reaching its limit or is being cut.

Short term cash injections to cover a large order perhaps and 'One off' large contracts

The Bank has said "no"

Peer to Peer Lending

How does peer-to-peer lending work?

Peer to peer is sometimes known as social lending or lend-to-save. Peer-to-peer lending or peer to business lending works by individual savers and borrowers coming together to get better rates. The advantage to the lender is that, in most cases, the amount they lend is spread over a number of investment opportunities giving them a greater chance of a successful return.

In May 2012 the UK Government committed to investing £100m in alternative lending including peer to peer-to-peer. This was to effectively by pass the banks and their reluctance to lend.

By July 2012 this form of lending had exceeded £300m and while currently self-regulated the Financial Conduct Authority will be the regulator from April 2014. So, as you can see, this is now a very valid source of funding.

Normal lending criteria such as credit scores and ability to pay back the loan still apply. However, the fact that you will at least get a hearing is an improvement.

The advantage to the borrower is flexible finance at competitive rates and no early repayment penalties. Added to this loan quotes do not impact on your credit score.

Recently one of the largest peer to peer lending sites, Zopa has announced a fund called safeguard that will pay out if borrowers fail to pay. Www.zopa.com

Crowd Funding

A fairly new but nonetheless exciting addition to the funding packages available. It relies principally on social networks and online communities to both publicise and encourage investment. Although it seems like a new way of funding a business any company with shareholders is, to some extent crowd funded.

There are currently three principal methods of crowd funding.

1. Equity Based Crowd Funding: Investors receive a stake in the company, basically you own a percentage of the business and if it is successful you get a share of that success.

2. Lending Based Crowd Funding: Investors are repaid for their investment over a period of time.

3. Reward Based Crowd Funding: Investors receive a tangible item or service in return for their funds.

Basically you go to a crowd funding site with your idea and business plan. If it is agreed that it is suitable for crowd funding a campaign will be set up and the bid posted on the web site.

Reward Based

You offer people incentives to invest in your business. For instance if you were starting or expanding a jewellery business you would offer an item of jewellery to anyone who invests. The item would depend on the investment made.

As an example, for £10 you may get a small item, for £20 something a little better and so on. If you can offer a bespoke piece you can make this your top incentive for whatever you feel is a fair amount.

This means that legally you are giving people something for their money

Before you start you will have to agree a target amount. Let's say £5,000. This will be made up by a selection of the investment amounts that you have put in place. You must reach the target in the set time otherwise the funding bid will be deemed to have failed. Some sites use a specific Pay Pal account where the money is held until the full amount is achieved. Failure to do so means that the money pledged to the account will not be taken. This prevents people investing in a project that does not go forward.

Once in place the work really starts the funding campaign will normally run for 60 days and you will have to constantly advertise by Facebook, tweeting and Linkedin. Ensure your friends pass on the information by posting likes or re-tweeting. Of course your own contact list is a valuable source of investment and often a quick phone call explaining what you are doing and why you require the money will pay dividends.

If your project is successful and raises the required amount you can draw down the money and proceed.

Crowd funding can be used more than once. You can use it to fund particular projects, marketing or research and development.

By offering the reward for the investment you have two advantages the money is effectively yours and the investors have no further claim on you or the money.

Finally it also acts as very useful marketing tool. If you raise your funding by using the product or service as a reward it helps to illustrate to other forms of finance that people are willing to pay for them. You can have a look on www.fundingcircle.com or try www.bloomvc.com with whom I have dealt and found to be very helpful and above all enthusiastic and well suited to small business.

Crowd Funding and Equity

This is a whole different animal and as the name suggests involves you passing on equity or shares in your business in exchange for investment. In itself not a problem, however, with what could be multiple investors decision making could be a problem.

A recent report by Glasgow Chamber of Commerce suggests that the sums being sought by smaller businesses is between £5,000 and £50,000. This makes Crowd Funding an attractive possibility.

For instance if you have a need for more funding and have grown to a point where larger equity partners are required you will find that instead a few equity holders having to make the decision you could have hundreds.

Bear in mind that equity crowd funding is not covered by the Financial Conduct Authority. All in all perhaps one to be avoided.

Donation-based Crowd Funding

Although charity rather than business based it is another example of how crowd funding works, the crowd gives money or some other resource because they want to support the cause. A good example is a junior football team which is raising money to travel to a tournament.

The crowd gives money and gets nothing in return, other than the good feeling that comes with knowing the team can travel to compete.

Business Angels or Venture Capitalists What's the Difference?

Venture Capitalists have been around for a long time and usually have access to large amounts of money, often raised through investors in the Venture Capital Company. They will probably want a seat/s on the board to protect the investment.

All of this requires a lengthy due diligence process so you will not get a quick decision.

Venture Capitalists will want to invest considerable sums of money so, in most cases this will not be an avenue that most small businesses will want to travel.

Business Angels are usually wealthy individuals. They will have great connections and in general will use their own money.

They do not operate under the restraints of Venture Capitalists and won't be looking for representation on the board. In general they are not keen in putting in a lot of capital.

They have a good understanding that in many cases the idea they are being asked to fund may be experimental in nature. The decision will, in most cases, be quick. Often a single meeting will be enough.

In the end you would go to whatever solution suits you best. If you are "experimenting" with a service or product an angel is probably better suited. However if you have a proven service or product and you have identified a solid market for it perhaps a Venture

Capitalist may be your better choice. They will supply greater resources especially as they can bring expertise and time to the table.

Pension Led Funding

There are options available which allow you to access your pension pot such as investing in the businesses intellectual property under a SIPP (Self Invested Pension Plan). This is an option open to Directors of companies so is only available if you are set up as a LTD company.

The pension fund either uses the intellectual property as security to borrow from the fund or buys it outright.

This fairly high risk if the firm hits a bad spell, inevitably, the value of the intellectual property is likely to fall so careful planning is required.

It should never be used as a last resort to try and save a business, it should only be used as an investment tool which will pay off for both the business and the pension.

It must be viewed, firstly, as an investment for the pension fund rather than a means of financing the business. It has to be done in the expectation that the value of the intellectual property will rise.

Methods to Avoid

Many small business owners are tempted to use their personal credit cards to tide them over. This is understandable, especially in a crisis. At all costs try to avoid doing this the cost is horrendous and basically what you are doing is lending the business the money. You have to be very specific about how you do this If not then HMRC will be asking questions when you try and recover the money.

Pay day loan companies have now entered the business market place. This reinforces the failure of the normal banking system to be fund enterprise if these companies can see a niche.

I would suggest that under no circumstances should you go down this route. No matter how desperate things may be this will only multiply your troubles.

Chapter 6

Who has their hand in your pocket?

One of the first things you will discover when you start your own business is the number of people who will try and separate you from your money. Unfortunately many of these will be legal and above board and I will deal with them later on in this guide.

It is the sneaky underhand illegal ways that scammers will use to get money from you that are the real cause for concern.

Nigerian Scam

Perhaps the most well - known is the Nigerian email. What happens is you receive an email from, usually the "widow" of a Government or military figure from Nigeria. In the course of their lifetime they have amassed a considerable amount of money. The "widow" is now keen to transfer the money out of the country and requires your help to do this. If you give them your bank details they will deposit the money in your account and then transfer it on. For your trouble they will pay you a commission of up to 20%. Given the sort of sums they are talking about this would amount to a considerable payment. If you agree the next email will be to ask you for a small sum up front to smooth the way in getting the bank transfer passed. This can be as much as £4,000, no matter you are going to get ten times that back, aren't you?

I would never fall that for that I can hear you all cry. However, I have, in my experience spoken to at least one small businessman who had paid said £4,000 so it is not impossible. The system works by sending out millions of the emails and if only a tiny proportion of people comply they have made a nice sum of money. Even just by giving them your bank details you are opening yourself up to fraud.

They are relying on either the recipient's greed or the fact that being a small business in difficult times you might take the chance to make some easy money. It might be enough to save your business, for instance.

Firstly if it seems too good to be true it is! Never pass on your bank details to anyone you have no knowledge of! Never, ever pay money up front. Most times if you do you will never see it again.

European City Guide

Although I am using the European City Guide here there are a series of other, similar, scams all using the same modus operandi.

What happens is you get a letter from the "guide" with a slip with your details at the bottom and a note to send it back to confirm your details are correct or the opportunity to change them if required. A great many businesses go ahead and do this. What they don't pick up on is a very small condition stating that by sending this back you are agreeing to pay to be part of the said guide.

Having sent the slip back, you think no more about it until an invoice arrives thanking you for your order and can we have 400 Euro please. At this point many small business owners panic, some pay others put it in the drawer and hope it goes away.

Do not pay them a single penny, they will bombard you for up to 18 months with ever increasing threat levels do not pay. I have never known them to follow up on their threats of court action. The threats are computer generated through a mass email system and are designed to cause enough fear that you pay up, again do not pay.

Check out Richard Corbett MEP at
http://www.richardcorbett.org.uk/stopecg.htm

This is a simple scam by automatically sending out millions of forms and invoices a tiny percentage return is all that is required to make it viable. Aimed at businesses, in the most part, that have accounts departments. When they see the demands the bulk of them will pay believing the invoices to be legitimate. The smaller businesses are caught in the net and as long as you hold firm you will be fine. The repeated demands are worrying and tiresome, shred them.

Overpayment of an invoice

This is an old favourite but still quite successful. You will get an order, more often than not from abroad. This will be an order from a new customer who will indicate that if all is well with this particular order then more business will follow.

The order will be placed and a cheque or draft will be sent on receipt of a pro forma invoice. Shortly after this you get a call saying they have ordered the wrong amount or some other error that means that the payment you have received is now more than the order.

They ask you to refund the money by return. You are keen to develop a relationship with this new customer so send refund via an electronic transfer. Then the original cheque or draft fails to get paid and you are now out of pocket.

What to do? Always be wary of new customers especially from abroad as this often gives them the extra clearing time on the draft they send you. Do not send any refund until you have their funds cleared in your account. If the order is of a reasonable size arrange an irrecoverable letter of credit.

Out of the Country!

This is a scam where initially all appears well, it is one I have personal experience of. You will receive a response to an advert, usually via email, asking about the product and generally expressing an interest.

You respond with more details and receive a response saying they wish to buy the item or product. You email back an invoice and then you get a reply saying that they are actually out of the country and what they are purchasing is actually a gift for a boyfriend/girlfriend etc who is working abroad once you have received "payment" from the customer. It is a scam and you will find that any payment will fail.

This scam is quite obvious once you know what you are looking for. The email will seem slightly odd in the way it reads. The grammar may be a bit off. For instance I was selling a car and was asked if the "auto" was still for sale, this should set alarm bells ringing. Often they ask the price even when it is clear on the advert what the price is. This is because it is an electronically manufactured email that is sent out to lots of people and fills in the item automatically. If you respond you will often then being emailed by a person who is attempting to complete the scam.

At this point cease communication. The intention is that you send you the item direct to the intended recipient abroad.

Banking Phone Scam

- A cold call, supposedly from someone in a position of authority/management warning of alleged fraudulent activity on your account or using your card(s),
- They may ask you to confirm some basic details – address and date of birth for example,
- They will explain that you need to contact your bank/card provider urgently, and suggest you hang up and call immediately,
- You will hang up and dial your bank/card provider,
- There may or may not be a dial-tone,
- The operator will ask you for your security details; PINs and 3 digit security codes for cards, usernames and passwords for online banking, and details from any multi-factor authentication tool you may have been issued – like a digital key fob or token,
- They will keep you on the line, potentially asking for this information multiple times, suggesting they need it to refund fraudulent transactions.

These calls can last hours, so that the fraudster can perform multiple transactions on your account.

This fraud is perpetrated by land-lines not disconnecting if only the recipient hangs up, you are then still talking to the fraudster not your bank/card provider; in this instance there would be no dial tone, however fraudsters may play a recorded dial tone to give the impression a new line has connected and you are calling your bank/card provider.

You are then divulging all your security details to them and they can transact freely with those details.

Banks and card providers may, from time to time, call you about possible fraud on your account but they will not ask for all your security details, the PIN for your card for example. If you receive a cold call about possible fraud, take the following action:

- **Do** be suspicious of cold calls; does the story ring true? How would the caller

- **Did** they get your home number if they are from a store, for example? Are they asking more security information than normal?

- **Don't** divulge card details like the PIN or 3 digit security code,

- **Don't** provide details from multi-factor authentication tools, like digital fobs, that you do not normally reveal when dealing with your bank,

Do hang up and call your bank/card provider from a different land-line or mobile phone if you receive a call like this – they will not mind if they have genuinely called you, and if was a fraudulent call you can alert your bank and they can check your account.

Phishing

Phishing is what it says the scammers send out dummy emails in the name of banks or building societies to "fish" for information. Many of these emails look very real and when you click the required link appear to take you to the banks web site. This is, of course a clone.

The message usually takes the form of telling you that access to your accounts has been frozen until you can reaffirm your security. You are then asked to go to the link in the message and input your security details to allow the account to operate as normal.

Clearly if you do not have an account with the "bank" sending you the email you will realise this is a scam. However it may seem to come from your bank. If it does **do not** click on anything or give any information, forward the email to your local trading standards then delete it. Quite simply, banks will not ask you for your full security information by email neither will they call you. If in any doubt phone your bank. You can find your nearest Trading Standards via. https://www.gov.uk/find-local-trading-standards-office

HMRC Tax Refunds

Around deadline dates of 31st October and 31st January is a common time for fraudsters to send out emails purporting to be from HMRC informing you that their records show you are due a tax refund. This is a sample of what you may receive.

Date: 29/10/2012

After the last annual calculations of your fiscal activity we have determined that you are eligible to receive a tax refund of 1840.00 GBP.

A refund can be delayed for a variety of reasons. As example, for submitting invalid records or applying after the deadline.

To access the form of your tax refund please click here

Please submit a tax refud request and allow us 3-7 days in order to process it.

Thank you

Bob Parsons

Tax Credit Office

You will be asked to put in your bank account details in order that the refund can be processed and put into your account. Your bank account will be emptied. HMRC does not send out emails informing people of tax rebates they only do this by mail.

If you get an email like this forward it to HMRC and then delete it. Remember "Too good to be true!"

Paying for services you can get free

This is a very common "scam" I put it in inverted commas because it is not a scam in the true sense of the word. Just because they are charging for services you can get free does not make it illegal but it is worth checking out if you are approached.

One of the most common manifestations of this particular ploy is Rates Rebates. Usually on or around revaluation time you will be called or visited by a salesman who will tell you that for an upfront fee of, say, £350 his company will appeal your rates and get them reduced.

Two things here, firstly never and I mean never pay for a service in advance. Secondly you can appeal your rates on your own at no cost.

Often the pitch is they will return the fee from the reduction they will win for you. It is not always possible to get any reduction for a variety of reasons but there is no refund as they have tried on your behalf.

Fortunately, in Scotland, with the Small Business Bonus Scheme which allows businesses with a rateable value of less than £10,000 to pay no rates this has somewhat reduced the attractiveness of this service.

Police Handbook Scam

This is a variation on the European City Guide. You will get a call or receive an invoice telling you that the advert you ordered is now ready for payment.

When you question it they will tell you they have a recording of you or a member of your staff agreeing to your placement of an advert. Ask for a copy of a recording. Often it transpires that they have phoned and asked if you "would be interested" in placing an advert.

You may have, innocently, said you would consider it and thought no more about it.

Obviously the scam is that this has nothing to do with the police and if printed will just be a list of adverts. Many people agree as they believe they are supporting their local police force. If you have fallen victim to this type of sale write to them explaining why you will not pay the bill and send a copy to trading standards in your area and if you have the information the trading standards of the area they are operating in.

The Bogus Invoice

In some ways it is similar to the handbook scam. It is probably the most blatant and crude scam. Often an invoice is sent for a small advert although some sort of service can be used instead. This is a very hit and miss but often works because if they keep the amount busy small business owner may pay it without thinking. If the company is large enough to have an accounts department the chances of payment are even greater. As I have said the amounts tend to be small, however, with millions of such invoices being sent it all adds for the scammers.

The Authorisation Scam

As with the Police hand book scam this involves adverts. Basically someone will call looking for details of people who can authorise advertisements. Then a short time later a further call is made to one of the people they have details for and indicate they have provisional agreement from the other person so the contact, thinking all is well, agrees to the advert.

This of course only works if they do not check with the other person. In a busy company, often this is not done. Again this is crude but often effective. The secret of both this and the previous Invoice Scam is keeping the amounts relatively small so as not to require any further authorisation before payment.

Data Protection Register

You will receive a letter from a company purporting to be an official body and asking for £100 to ensure you are registered for data protection under the 1998 act.

This is a requirement but costs £35 via the correct body which is the Information Commissioners Office. Depending upon the size of the company and to what extent they process the data they may be exempt. For more information, visit the ICO website at www.ico.org.uk or call the helpline on 0303 123 1113.

Business Directories

These fall into the same category as the City Guides scams. You receive a letter with a slip asking you to confirm your details.

Health and Safety Registration

Small businesses are targeted by bogus "agencies" demanding a fee to ensure registration. This not a requirement in general, you may need to have license for other specific services but this can be easily checked at the HSE website www.HSE .gov.uk

Microsoft Security Issues

This can take two guises. Firstly the direct call informing you that they are either Microsoft or a Microsoft Certified and they are aware of a problem with your PC. They will then ask for remote access to the computer. Obviously this is not an option, you cannot have anyone having access to your PC and your details.

If you have or a member of your staff has given access details, change your password immediately.

Secondly when you open up Internet Explorer you will get a message telling you the computer is infected and to run the link to the scanner. By doing this you will add to the problem and also asked for payment to clean the computer.

Basically there is nothing to be cleaned but it is now very difficult to get rid of the scanner.

The only way to do so is to download onto a USB on a separate PC a program called Malware Bytes. Plug this into the infected system and run the Malware program from the USB.

These are small selection of the types of scams that can be perpetrated on your business in an effort to part you from your hard earned cash. So, what can you do to help to protect yourself?

The Corporate Telephone Preference Service (TPS)

This is a free service and should ensure that you will reduce calls. It will not stop the real rogues but it is a start.

Publishing/marketing company 'anti-scam' questionnaire

There are questions to ask if you are contacted by cold callers. Hopefully it will let you make a more informed decision.

1. What is your name?

2. What is the name of your company?

3. What is your contact number?

4. How did you get my details?

5. Where is your company based? Get full address. Beware PO box numbers

6. What is the name of the magazine/guide/directory/publication that I would be advertising in?

7. What type of publication is it?

8. How many copies will be printed?

9. Where will they be distributed or circulated? Get post code areas to ensure it is relative to the locality you trade in. This particularly important if you are a retail outlet.

10. Who will distribute the publication? How will they distribute it and over what time scale?

11. Can I get to see a proof copy?

12. Is the publication being produced on behalf of another organisation?

13. If YES, what is the name and address of that organisation?

14. Is that organisation or your company a registered charity?

15. If YES, what is the registered number of the charity?

16. If I agree to place an advert, what percentage of the cost will go to that charity?

All in all be aware. Take nothing at face value if it is not a company you have dealt with in the past. Not everyone is out to scam you but in these difficult times taking an extra step to check things out can pay dividends.

Chapter 7

H.R. And running a small business.

The vast majority of small businesses in the UK employ ten or less people. A high proportion of them will be so small they will either have no employees or just a couple.

I have already said that they are also, currently, the most underrated source of new jobs. With a little targeted help there is an opportunity for many more jobs to be created.

Small businesses perceive HR and the attendant employment law as a minefield that they would rather not navigate. Given that small businesses have the capacity to be employers it needs to be addressed.

The cost of running an HR department is out with the budget of most small companies with most owners not having the relevant HR knowledge, so taking on an employee becomes both onerous and fearful.

The media hype up all the negatives in current employment law, and there are more than a few, this inhibits possible small employers.

Most of you will have to "buy" in your HR support at least in the first instance. There are a number of ways you can do this. The first and most obvious one is to bring in a consultant as when you need them.

The key word here is choice. Ensure that the advisor that you pick truly understands how small businesses work. Many so called experts have only experienced HR at a corporate level and try to apply those solutions to the SME.

This will not work. The dynamics in a small business are such that even the smallest issues can have a huge knock on effect. For instance if you employ ten people or less and you have a personality clash or often just a minor disagreement the effect on staff morale can be considerable.

In a larger business this kind of clash can be managed much more easily by keeping the factions apart, this is much less likely to be possible in a small company.

How do you balance having enough staff to ensure the business runs effectively without cutting into your bottom line?

Perhaps by starting a part time employee in the beginning, training them up and then re-assessing the role to see if it justifies an upgrade to full time.

Be sure of the type of employee you want. Do you want someone with experience or would you rather train someone your self, this often allows for a better fit in a small company.

There are a lot of incentives out there to encourage you to employ people. This incentive is most often by way of part payment of wages. While this may seem attractive in the first instance be aware of the hoops and extra administration you will be liable for.

Many if not all the schemes offering financial help will be steering you to a specific group of people. Young persons or longer term unemployed, being the most prevalent currently.

While this laudable in its approach it does not best suit the needs of small businesses and should be approached with some caution. Unless the financial assistance being offered is key to your decision be prepared to look at the applicants as critically as you would were the finance not a driver.

Recent surveys have shown that the financial imperative is not always the guiding factor when a small business employs. Suitability and general attitude are considered to be more important.

Remember our earlier points regarding how a new employee fits into the new role and how the will interact with others.

The steps required when employing someone in the UK.

Your first decision should be what are you prepared to pay for the vacancy. You must pay the **minimum wage**. For the current rates you should check at https://www.gov.uk/national-minimum-wage/who-gets-the-minimum-wage

You have an obligation to ensure that the person you are employing is legally entitled to work in the UK. Again you can check at https://www.gov.uk/legal-right-to-work-in-the-uk

You will need to put **Employers Liability Insurance** in place, speak to your insurer to get the best deal.

Within the first two months of employing someone you will have to give the new employee a **Contract of Employment**. This does not need to be overly sophisticated. It should include rate and frequency of pay, working hours including shift patterns if applicable. Also required will be start date and job title with a brief description. Holiday entitlement should form part of the contract or agreement.

You must register with HMRC as an employer
http://www.hmrc.gov.uk/payerti/getting-started/register.htm

Wage or Salary slips

When paying your staff you must give staff a statement showing clearly all deductions including National Insurance, Income Tax, Pension and student loan repayments.

You must abide by the **Working Time** Directive. Employees are only required to work a maximum average of 48 hours per week based over a calculation period of 17 weeks.

What are working hours? This is time when the worker is available to carry out the employers tasks. Lunch hours and breaks are not considered working time.

For "on call" workers the rule is that if you are at your place of employment and available it counts. If you are free to be elsewhere and do other things it does not.

The employee can volunteer to not be bound by the directive. They cannot be forced into this and there must be a form of written agreement.

Holidays

The law requires that workers get a minimum of 5.6 weeks holiday each year. This can include public holidays. An employee has a right to holidays from the commencement of their employment. Entitlement should be that for each month worked you are entitled to a twelfth of your annual entitlement.

When it comes to timing you have reasonable control over this. You can, for instance close for two weeks a year and everyone has to take their holiday at that time. You must be reasonable in allowing holidays and staff should understand why and how you make the decisions. A holiday chart is an excellent idea.

Break Time

Every employee is required to have a twenty minute break in each six hour period. They should have a consecutive eleven hours rest between shifts every day. A worker is entitled to one day off per week.

The working time regulations are governed by the Health and Safety Executive.

Chapter 8

Compliance

Compliance, with the plethora of regulation is a constant thorn in the side of small businesses. Red tape can strangle fledgling enterprises and severely restrict even the most efficient company.

The reason for this takes us back to an earlier chapter where we discuss the inability of Government and their agencies to really understand what a small business is. By taking the UK definition as being less than 250 employees, the problem starts to become clear.

Most, if not all, legislation tends to be designed with the larger company in mind. They have the resources and in house professionals to deal with this on a day to day basis.

No account is taken of size or ability to deal with regulation and in most cases the small company has to comply at exactly the same level as the larger one.

Many small businesses will break the law on a daily basis and be completely unaware that they are doing so.

Compliance with the standard requirements such as HMRC and the Health and Safety Executive are well covered by the government websites. However you still have to make the time to ensure you are complying. Plus the legislation changes often and updates issued. There are some websites they specialise in monthly updates, usually tailored to your specific requirements but at a cost. Have a look at www.legislationupdateservice.co.uk (if you are one of Business Sorted monthly clients you will be kept up to date on major employment law changes)

Health and Safety

You have to be aware of all the Health and Safety issues such as Fire Safety, have you the right extinguisher? This will depend on the type of business and the class of fire likely in your normal day to day practices.

Electrical Safety, Requires checking of overall wiring condition, load on various sockets, defective equipment, poor insulation.

Repetitive Injury Strain (RSI), most common on people carrying out computer based work on a regular basis. Ensure you have correct breaks for staff to step away from the computer. Check height of desk and chair. Is there support for the wrist when typing or using the mouse?

These are just a few of the items you need to consider as part of your Health and Safety policy.

An excellent tool kit for small businesses put together by Healthy Working Lives and is available at

http://www.healthscotland.com/uploads/documents/20227-SafetyHealthWellbeingHealthProfits.pdf

Real Time Reporting with HMRC

This has recently been put in place by HMRC and is a system where every time you pay an employee the Pay as you Earn details must be submitted electronically. If you normally pay staff on a weekly basis you will be required to do it weekly. Likewise if monthly then details must be submitted monthly.

The original deadline for compliance was extended for businesses of less than 50 employees to October 2013, was then extended to April 2013.

You will be required to purchase the software to allow you do this and also be responsible for having a good broadband connection, in some areas this may prove to be a problem, particularly in rural areas where there are known issues with broadband and its reliability. In some very extreme cases you may have to copy the data to disc and forward it to a third party to ensure it is input into the HMRC system.

One of the issues is the lack of small business knowledge on the subject and an in a considerable proportion of instances no knowledge that the requirement exists.

Remembering earlier advice in the guide, speak to HMRC and ask for their help it is in their best interests for businesses to understand what is needed.

www.hmrc.gov.uk

Data Protection

It is easy to get caught out on this one as it seems shrouded in a great deal of misinformation. Under the 1998 Data Protection Act if you handle personal information about individuals you must protect that data.

The easiest way to ascertain whether or not you need to register is to go to the Information Commissioner's website and take the self - assessment test. They also offer a specific small business "Getting it Right Guide" which will give you the information that you need. It is better to check than fall foul of the regulations.
www.ico.org.uk

PCIDSS

Like Data Protection it is better to check than be caught out.

Payment Card Industry Data Security Standard. Following from the previous information on data protection this is one of the compliance issues that many small businesses either don't know about or do not fully understand.

You are required to meet the PCIDSS standards if you trade on line and take payments electronically. There are 12 basic security standards to ensure that you are not putting your customers at risk of fraud.

A compliance certificate may be required at a cost of £75.00 - £100 per year. However, if you only transact via a third party such as World-pay or Pay Pal you do not require this. Only if any transaction is completed on your website do you need to have a compliance certificate.

You still have to be compliant if you accept credit card payments and have a merchant number but complete off site. There are some forms to complete and a few safety procedures put in place. (Business Sorted monthly clients can access free advice on PCIDSS via our partners Card -line)

Go to www.pciwsecuritystandards.org where you will find reference guides and standard forms for you to use.

Playing Music on Your Premises

This is a huge bone of contention with many businesses not just small ones. Most are caught by the playing of radio music. If the general public cannot here the music you should be OK. However if they can you are liable to pay a fee. For instance if you have a radio on in the back shop for the employees you must ensure it cannot be heard beyond there. This includes being able to hear it for a brief time when the door is opened or closed.

Background music of any kind requires a license as does having a TV on for customers. The fee is due to not one but two organisations PPL (Phonographic Performance Ltd) and PRS for Music Ltd (Performing Rights Society).

This is a legal requirement under the Copyright, Design and Patents Act 1988.

While this is yet another expense on your business, if you play or intend to play music it is better to check what is required rather than be liable for any excess.

PPL

PPL is responsible for the licensing of recorded music either played in public or broadcast over TV, Radio or the internet. The fees charged vary according to premises and the amount of music being played. For instance a small shop will pay a small fee as compared to a dance studio.

A guide price is a shop with less than 600 Square Metres will pay £122.64

Contact www.ppluk.com

PRS

As a guide a shop with an audible area of up to 100 Square Metres will pay £151.00 per year.

However if you apply after you have started paying music there is a 50% surcharge on the first year bring it to £226.60.

This is a tricky area as most small businesses are oblivious to the need for such a license and only discover it is needed when a PRS representative comes calling and so are automatically in line to pay the higher rate. We suggest you attempt to strike a deal with them to get a reduced initial fee.

Contact www.prsformusic.com

Waste Transfer Notes

This gives details of waste being transferred between one person and another. For instance, when you have your trade waste collected it should be accompanied by a transfer note. It is not a standard design and many collectors produce their own.

What may happen is your collector will ask you if you wish them to supply and fill in the transfer note for which they will charge a fee.

You can download a SEPA example transfer note at http://www.netregs.org.uk/library_of_topics/waste/duty_of_care/complete_waste_transfer_notes.aspx and complete it yourself at no charge.

Zero Waste

Zero Waste Scotland are currently alerting businesses of the new regulations that are coming or have come into place. Your responsibilities are that you should:

- Apply the waste hierarchy to the management of your waste.
- From 1st January 2014 present glass, metal, plastic, paper and card (including cardboard) for separate collection.
- In some circumstances, present food waste for separate collection.
- Take care of the waste while you hold it for example during storage, so it does not escape from your control.
- Ensure your waste is collected by someone authorised to receive it, for example, a registered waste carrier or waste manager with the relevant authorisation.
- Ensure that the transfer of waste is covered by a waste transfer note including a full description of the waste and
retain a copy of this note for two years.

- Ensure that the waste description is accurate and contains all the information you are reasonably in a position to provide for safe handling, transport, treatment, recovery or disposal by subsequent holders.

Much of this, in a small business, will require some forward planning especially the need to keep metal, plastic, paper and card separately for collection. There are some cases where you are allowed to mix them.

This still appears a bit of a grey area as, if you co-mingle it must still "result in material of a high quality which can go forward to recycling" check with
www.zerowastescotland.org.uk

Unfortunately there is still some confusion and some instances of left hand – right hand syndrome.

A white goods retailer had to recycle the boxes and the packaging the products come in, he then takes them to the local recycling centre as and when he has a van load. The local council operate a flat charge scheme where they charge per load based on the size of van or truck being used. Our retailer uses a transit van and is charged the flat rate of £70. This applies whether the van is full or not.

To cut down on unnecessary costs he breaks down the packaging and ties in bundles to store at the back shop until he has a van load.

A common sense solution. He saves money and cuts down on the number of trips to the recycling centre. However the local fire service on a visit to the shop pointed out that by storing the cardboard he was creating a fire hazard and this was unacceptable.

There was no real satisfactory solution as neither the fire service nor the council were prepared to change their position. After a meeting with both sides we got an agreement that he could store up to a certain amount of packaging on site. This still means twice as many trips to the centre and twice as many flat rate charges. Not the perfect outcome but it does demonstrate that the best solution to a problem is to get all parties together and discuss what can be done.

Fire Safety Regulations

Anyone who has control to any extent of the premises will have some responsibilities for ensuring that those occupying the premises are safe from harm caused by fire.

Sounds a little scary doesn't it? Essentially you are required, by law, to carry out a Fire Risk Assessment. You have to identify any thing that could cause harm by fire. Much of this will be common sense.

There are five basic steps to carrying out an assessment:

    1 - Identify people at risk
    2 - Identify fire hazards
    3- Evaluate the risk and decide if existing fire safety measures are adequate
    4- Record fire safety risk assessment information
    5- Review of fire safety risk assessment

This information must be recorded if five or more people are employed, the premises are licensed or subject to registration or the enforcing authority has issued a notice requiring you to do this.

The assessment type will vary depending on the complexity of the premises and what you are doing on the premises. Clearly if you are making fireworks as opposed to selling insurance the risk will be much greater and require a more detailed approach.

An excellent source of notes and examples can be found at

http://www.scotland.gov.uk/Topics/Justice/public-safety/fire-and-rescue-services/FireLaw/GeneralGuidance/FireSafetyRiskAssessment

Chapter 9

Insurance?

Liability Insurance

Unless you are a sole trader and either do not employ anyone or only employ family members this is a legal requirement and comes in a few forms. There are mainly three types of risk. Firstly if you employ people you will need Employers' Liability Insurance. Volunteers, part-time workers and contractors count as employees. This will cover you if any member of staff should be injured or become ill when they are employed by you. The minimum cover, by law is £5m.

If you are working from premises and or customers will visit you at your place of business, this includes your home, you must have public liability insurance. This will cover you for any accidents. If you carry out work on a client's premises you are also covered. It is important to note that, particularly in the public sector, if you wish to do work for them you will have to have good liability cover. If you exhibit at trade shows or conferences this should be taken into account.

Product liability covers you if you make, sell or repair products usually up to a maximum of £2m.

Professional Indemnity Insurance

This is a wise policy to take out if you are in the business of giving any sort of advice. Consultants, for instance, would be well advised to ensure they are covered. You will be protected should you give inaccurate advice.

Many of the professional bodies require that you have it in place.

There are other professions or lines of work where specific insurance may be required. Scaffolders, roofers and welders, for instance, are examples of where specialised insurance will be required.

Home Insurance/Business Insurance

If you run a business from home do not assume that your home insurance will cover your equipment. Don't forget to check your car insurance policy for business use. For a small extra charge you can usually get the extra cover. Many companies offer a homeworkers policy specifically designed to suit this eventuality.

Business Interruption

Depending on your circumstances an interruption policy can be useful. What would you do if fire or flood or a break in affected your ability to do business? It is well worth investigating.

Most policies will cover you for loss of earnings or profit. This is particularly useful in cases where a third party action or event disrupts your ability to do business and earn money.

Key Person Insurance

This can often be allied to the above and is particularly important in a smaller businesses.

If you have a member of staff who is vital to the continued running of the company it can be very beneficial to consider this type of insurance.

Credit Insurance

This type of policy covers you for bad debt due to a customer going out of business or defaulting on payment. It may not be worthwhile to take on an overall policy, however, it is worth considering if you have a large contract to fulfil and it accounts for a significant proportion of your turnover. Also worth bearing in mind that most policies will only pay out a maximum of 80% of the total loss.

Directors and Managers Insurance

If you are a manager or director of a company you are legally exposed to unlimited personal liability. The Companies Act of 1985 and 1989 enforces around 200 statutory liabilities, so, worth consideration.

Chapter 10 HMRC – Tax and VAT

As already stated in other sections of the guide HMRC, who cover both Tax and VAT, are one of the agencies you should work closely with. Always pay on time and if you have a problem tell them. They have a range of courses to cover most eventualities.

An Inspector Calls

Recent legislation means that the inspectors may call at any time and this will include those working from home. It is now much more likely that you will be inspected than it has been in the past. How do you deal with an inspection?

Ideally you will have the foresight to ensure you have protection against such an occurrence either by buying insurance or joining an organisation such as the Federation of Small Businesses who offer this as a right of membership. By having this in place you will save yourself a great deal of time and grief, assuming you have done nothing wrong.

If you are in the position of having to tackle an inspection alone there are some key points to remember. Firstly it will be long and tedious and things you never imagined were the tax man's business will suddenly be so. This is particularly true if you are a sole trader or not a limited company. You will be asked to supply information on drawings, how much you spend on the weekly shop, not even your wife's hair appointments are sacrosanct.

Secondly you are guilty until you prove yourself innocent, if the tax man decides that you owe £10,000 you have to prove you do not.

When actually dealing with the tax man be open and upfront and get a good advisor from the outset. Ensure when you have to meet with HMRC you are as well prepared as you can.

If you have, for any reason, underpaid, make a reasonable offer of repayment bearing in mind that interest will be due on any tax owing from the date it should have been paid.

Lastly if you are due back tax, pay it and do not fall behind again. If HMRC see a second "offence" you will be treated much more harshly the second time.

PAYE (Pay as You Earn)

If you employ people this the way you will pay the tax and national insurance. You will have to keep correct and accurate records for each employ and pay the tax you collect timeously. Soon you will be required to electronically tell the tax man each time you pay an employee this called Real Time Information. In principal, this should make the collection of tax by the employer simpler and take away the need for end of year returns.

VAT

First of all you need to decide whether or not you should register for VAT. If you expect that your turnover will exceed £79,000 per year or it has done so it the past twelve months you are required to be registered.

You can also become VAT registered voluntarily. You may wish to do this if the bulk of your turnover is with other VAT registered businesses. Once you are registered you will be required to fill in a VAT return, this will usually be done quarterly. In its simplest form you show the VAT you have charged on your sales or output tax and you show the VAT you have paid on your purchases or input tax.

HMRC are then paid the difference. In the event the input exceeds the output you will receive a refund from HMRC.

Remember treat the tax man as a friend and keep him appraised if everything that is happening, by doing this he is in the best position to help you

www.hmrc.gov.uk

Chapter 11

Small Business Big Problems

Running a small business, as we have already said, can be very rewarding it will also often mean dealing with a series of problems. Many will be simple day to day issues that can easily be resolved with a minimum of time and disruption.

The more significant problems that all businesses, large and small, will experience will have a more detrimental effect on the smaller business. Why is this? Larger companies have better resources by way of staff and in house expertise to deal with most of the problems that can come their way. If you are a small business the problem often requires to be dealt with by the owner. Depending on the issue at hand, this will mean valuable time being spent dealing with the problem and being available to run the business.

Often a Catch 22 situation develops, where the business owner tries to juggle with the problem and run the day to day business. The more time given over to trying to resolve the issue can lead to other problems because their attention is elsewhere. Mostly they will not have the in house experience of the larger business or the expert knowledge on how to deal with the issue or who best to approach. Very often an inordinate amount of time is wasted at the start of the process just attempting to find out who you should be directing your questions to in order to start making inroads.

Obviously not all problems or queries fall into this category I'm talking, for example, about disagreements with your bank, utility company, local authority, the tax man, suppliers and landlords to name just a few.

Local authorities are often the most irksome as they seem to have special training in avoiding the issue and passing the buck. The earlier remarks about where to direct your questions or where to seek advice or redress are particularly apposite in this instance. With your local council being responsible for a myriad of things that directly affect your business the impact of any delay can be damaging. You have licensing, of all sorts, planning, road repairs not to mention economic development. Many councils are adept at displaying the "Left Hand not knowing what the Right Hand is doing" style of internal management. As we look at a number of actual cases of problem dealing/solving I will show you how to circumvent many of the barriers put in your way.

If the problem requires time and expertise you will often be better outsourcing the management of said problem. It is important to consider, from the outset, just how much time you, personally would have to dedicate to the problem, with the added codicil that you may not have the immediate knowledge to cut short the process. An outside expert will have this skill and experience. While there is an upfront cost for such a service this needs to be balanced against the time you will take away from concentrating on your core aim, making a living, and the stress that often ensues when trying to resolve a problem.

By using an experienced business consultant you will, almost certainly reach a resolution in a much shorter time. This is because any consultant worth their salt will have a range of contacts across all the aforementioned institutions and will know exactly who to go to in the initial stages.

The range of problems and issues we will cover will give you a broad range of instances and solutions that you can apply to your own particular problems. The solutions and ideas in these particular accounts are to be considered as a guide only, each situation is different and not all the circumstances will apply across the board.

In order to make reference as simple as possible I have grouped the examples under the auspices of who is causing the problem, for instances banks utilities etc. Some of the issues will be similar but because of the institution being dealt with the approach may differ.

Banks

Case1

When businesses are asked to give examples of the types of ongoing issues that they have to deal with most frequently their dealings with their bank are at or close to the top of the list.

I believe this is due to a number of circumstances. At the early stages of this guide I make a point of ensuring that you always appraise your bank of any problems you have or expect to have. I have also said banks don't like surprises. It is important to remember those two key points and in doing so you will, hopefully, remove some of the problems and frictions before they appear. If you give your bank a reason to doubt you, they will and getting back their faith will take time.

Having said that, in my experience, it is the banks themselves that often initiate the problems. In recent times they have removed local account managers. The person who visited your premises knew you and your business. In my opinion by going down this route it is the cause of many misunderstandings and grief. Some of the major banks have gone as far as centralising all their account managers. This means you will probably never meet them face to face and your dealings will be by phone. Others have gone to a half - way house approach where one account manager covers a post code or number of post codes. In Scotland, for instance, this can work reasonably well in the heavily populated central belt but becomes completely impractical when the areas are more rural. A good example is the bank who removed their island branch manager and based them in Oban. This was done by post code allocation with no thought to the practicalities of how the arrangement would work. It meant a 2 hour ferry trip and depending on timings an overnight stay. This kind of arrangement does not lend itself to a successful partnership with the bank.

Because of the recent economic crisis banks have become extremely risk averse and in some cases would rather cut their perceived losses than offer the little extra support that would help a company survive and in the process keep local jobs in place.

This case is a good example. The business is a small manufacturing company with a fairly large overdraft and the bank holds a floating charge over the property and the debtor book.

They are going through a sticky patch but have orders finally coming in but they realise they are going to have to rationalise, find some extra working capital and make some people redundant to lower the ongoing overheads.

They have a piece of land along the side of the plant that they have a cash offer worth about half of the outstanding overdraft.

Unfortunately the initial position of the bank is to allow it go ahead but only if all the proceeds are used to reduce the overdraft. It has been pointed out to the account managers that this will result in the closure of the business and the loss of some 30 jobs.

When I was approached by the company to try and broker a deal that would satisfy the banks need for overdraft reduction and allow them to continue trading and save the bulk of the jobs I sat down with the owners to ensure I had all the information required and that I could approach the issue from a neutral point of view.

Having checked the figures and order book it was clear that the bank were taking the position that while they would still have the remainder of the overdraft they could make up the difference if they actioned the floating charge.

In this situation the bank took the view that with the floating charge over the remaining property and the debtor book they would get their money back, the business owner getting the remainder. They took no account of the fact that up to 30 people would be unemployed with subsequent effect on the local economy not that the business had contracts on the books but did not have the working capital to fulfil them.

In terms of cold hard logic the bank are only interested in ensuring their position is safe. In this case, with floating charge, they were still in a strong position no matter which way the decided to go. The problem is that account managers are being given instructions to reduce the bank's exposure to businesses and there are even bonuses in place to encourage this attitude.

I arranged a meeting with a senior account manager and laid out where I felt their proposed action was inappropriate given the knock on effect on the local economy and by putting 30 people out of work the bank would appear to be acting in the best interests of their shareholders rather than supporting local, viable businesses.

After considerable negotiation it was agreed that around 75% would be used to reduce the overdraft with the remaining £providing the cash to, unfortunately, make a few people redundant and provided the required working capital to complete the orders. The redundancies were essential in order to rationalise the overheads.

The lesson to be learned here is to always go above the account manager allocated to you. They have to work to very rigid guidelines and do not have the authority to be more flexible. Before you meet with the bank always ensure you have your facts and figures correct and clearly laid out. In addition a written submission showing the reasons for you requesting any decision to be reviewed.

In the submission accentuate all the positive reasons but don't forget to highlight any negatives and how you intend to approach and deal with them, remember banks and surprises.

Case 2

This instance is not so much about how the bank has acted, which in some ways is entirely reasonably. It is about ensuring that if you have any internal or external connections, formal or otherwise with other businesses on which your own banking needs and decisions are based that you need to be clear how it all impinges on your direct banking agreement.

The company had a fairly substantial overdraft with one of the large banks. Out of the blue they were contacted and told that the overdraft facility was being cut without any notice. This, clearly, was a blow to the cash flow of the company and the bank were being very reticent as to why they were doing so.

I approached a Senior Account Manager and queried the decision while making clear the detrimental effect to the business. It transpired that the company was part owned by another of the banks clients. Said business was in trouble and had its overdraft cut. The knock on effect was that the bank felt that this company would suffer because of this relationship an as a result decided to cut the overdraft limit. The business owner and I sat down with the bank and explained the adverse effect this would have and that this decision was making the situation worse. It was finally agreed that there would be a cut but only by 25%.

Sometimes it is connections or partnerships that affect your position with the bank. Something to be considered when entering to a business agreement.

Two similar cases now. Firstly a client with a small guest house was informed by the bank with a smallish overdraft that she must clear the overdraft as she was in breach of the original agreement because the through put of funds was below the level required. Again I spoke with the bank and they agreed that the overdraft could be converted to a loan and paid off over a period of time and the account operated in future on a credit basis.

Secondly a small local charity was informed that the account was being closed as, like the previous case, insufficient funds were going through the account. It was pointed out to the bank that this was a special case and it was good publicity for them to be seen to be supporting a local good cause.

Both of this instances show the importance of understanding the requirements of the account you have with the bank and that you should continue to monitor that you are fulfilling the conditions of the arrangement. If you realise that you are no longer doing this contact the bank and change to a different account. Remember banks and surprises.

Utilities

Utility companies are a constant source of irritation to many businesses and I am going to provide you with range of actual case studies that will cover Water, Gas, and Electricity etc.

The most common problem when dealing with a utility company is the complete inability to speak to the same person twice. This means that you have to go back to the beginning of the story each time you call. To attempt to stop this happening ask them for a reference number, any decent helpline should always have a system in place that allows them to track all contacts with the customer. I have to say in my experience this is not always the case. The reason for asking for some sort of reference is to try and force the issue. They will probably have an internal tracking system at the very least.

Remember the warning at the start of any call where they tell you they will be recording it for "training and security" purposes this can work both ways. Do not agree to anything verbally always insist on, at the least, an email confirmation. Be sure of your facts before you call.

I have known instances with some companies when they have been challenged about their recording, which you are entitled to a copy of, have clearly edited it to suit their version of events. This is not done by the large suppliers and is only occasionally a problem with some of the smaller suppliers. On the two occasions I have come across it has been small telecommunications companies when they have cold called the client and then made it appear that they have agreed to a contract. Never agree verbally to any cold call offer, remember minimum email confirmation of offer.

If you are having real problems it is worth considering recording the call yourself as a safety net.

Dealing with utility companies is a prime example where you will waste a great deal of time trying to resolve relatively straightforward issues. It makes the case for bringing in an experienced consultant to do it for you. You will save money in the longer term.

Energy Suppliers

The first example I am going to use is an excellent example of how some of the large utilities operate and their unbending belief that they are always right.

A recently opened café was approached after about a year by the energy supplier to say that they owed a significant sum of money after they had finally got round to reading the meter after many months estimated bills. The client was aghast at the sum being asked for around £11,000 this being on top of the normal payments already made.

I met with the café owner and it was pointed out by them that the supplier's figures were totally incorrect as they had been keeping a note of the meter readings on a weekly basis since day one. I approached the supplier and explained this and suggested we may dealing with a straight forward error or a faulty meter. Within a matter of days, when the business owner was out and with no prior warning, the meter was taken out and a replacement installed.

The supplier then issued a series of warnings including a threat to cut off the café. When I questioned them, not an easy proposition, and asked if the old meter was in fact faulty I was told they did not know as there was no record of what was wrong with the old meter.

The new meter meantime, while producing slightly higher figures than may be reasonably expected, did not produce the sort of usage that would result in the £11,000 bill over a similar period. The client was at their wits end and offered arbitration and to pay a sum equal to what the new meter would have produced over the same period. All to no avail the energy supplier point blank refused to admit anything was wrong. They did not answer emails or letters and phoning meant starting afresh with each new helpline contact.

We then approached OFGEM with a view to an enquiry and they too were met with the same arrogant stance and failed to produce any evidence or explain what happened to the essential evidence of the old meter.

In the end the strain and stress was overwhelming and the café closed, a perfectly good business ruined by intransigence.

Another instance which happens to also be a café. The owner was approached by a utility broker who told her based on the current usage they had a cheaper tariff that would suit the business. The rate would mean a monthly payment of between £30 and £45 per month. The deal was agreed and signed. Immediately there was problem. The monthly amount being taken was £140 per month. The client had complained bitterly over a period months without success. By this time they had run up a sum of around £550 in overpayments. I contacted the broker and went through the original contract with the area manager and they admitted that the £140 per month was an error.

I asked that they arrange to repay the £550 to the client and then ensure that the correct amount was then taken each month. They then informed the business owner that "legally" the most they could return in a lump sum was £200 the balance being in a series of payments from her normal monthly payments.

I again spoke with the area manager and told him in no uncertain terms that there was no legal imperative that limited the return of overpayments and that the client was to be reimbursed immediately. This duly happened and the café owner changed supplier at the first opportunity.

Always query any statements from suppliers that indicate they are acting in a certain manner because the law requires it. If you are getting no satisfaction from the helpline go to the area manager. If needs be approach OFGEM and threaten negative publicity in the local press.

A small hairdresser who had recently moved into new premises received a bill from a gas supplier for a standing charge for gas. He does not use gas! When he questioned the invoice he was told that there was a gas meter on the premises although it was disconnected this attracted a daily standing charge, the meter was situated behind a new wall that had been put up and was inaccessible.

When he queried this position further after he pointed out that he had no intention of ever using gas the answer was that the fact that the meter was in situ it gave him the option to have a gas. The energy company were then asked to remove meter, their reply was that they would be happy to do so but he would have to pay £400 + VAT for this to happen.

I contacted the gas supplier and pointed out the absurdity of this as a position after getting past the help (sic) desk to a more senior manager the matter was resolved and the meter was removed FOC.

The common thread with the last two examples is the need to speak to someone in a reasonably senior position. The normal help desk contacts, who I appreciate have a difficult job to do, have to work to a set of instructions and procedures in response to each particular problem, with no room for variance.

Rollover Contracts – These are prevalent in the utility market. You sign up to a favourable deal over a fixed period and in the small print it will say that at the end of the contract if you do not notify the company you will be rolled over onto a standard deal. This, often, will tie you up for a similar period to the initial deal.

OFGEM recently introduced new rules for micro businesses (has less than ten employees and an annual turnover below £2m).

When the initial contract is signed the terms and conditions must be fully explained. Within ten days of signature of a new or continuation contract you must get written copies.

Suppliers must let customers have sight of renewal terms around 60 days before the end of the current contract. They must show clearly what will happen if the contract is allowed to rollover or if the customer does not wish to rollover. You then have 30 days to negotiate a new deal. The most common error is that the business fails to act on the notice when it is sent out.

When you sign a fixed term contract go to your calendar and put in a reminder to yourself 3 months before the contract ends.

Utility Brokers –There are many excellent Utility Brokers out there who will find you the best independent deal for your business. I suggest checking them out as this can pay big dividends.

If you are approached and the deal sounds attractive, do nothing until you have done some basic checks. Look on the internet and see if the broker has been attracting bad reviews. Ask them directly if they are representing particular power companies.

Speak to their local Trading Standards office as this is where most complaints, if any exist, will have been made.

Any doubts go to OFGEM www.ofgem.gov.uk

As part of our Business Sorted monthly package we work with an experienced and trustworthy broker who will look at your utility bills as part of your deal.

Business Rates – If you operate from business premises you are required to pay Business Rates. The amount you pay will be based on what is known as the rate poundage times the current rateable value of your premises.

The rateable value is assessed every five years by the Scottish Assessor., this is based on a notional rental value of the shop or office.

The rates poundage is set every year by central government and is currently 46.2pence per pound of rateable value. If you have a rateable value of £25,000 you will pay £11,550 in business rates.

Over £10,000 and up to £12,000 you will receive a 50% discount. Over £12,000 up to £18,000 the discount is 25%.

It is important to note that the discount applies to the aggregated total of all premises in the business. If you have two shops, one with a rateable value of £6,000 and another at £5,500, you receive the discount on the combined total in this case 50% not two lots of 100%.

In Scotland, under the Small Business Bonus Scheme many businesses are exempt from paying any rates. All premises with a rateable value of less than £10,000 will pay no rates.

Water Charges – The most common calls I receive are regarding water charges. The main complaint is they are too high for the amount of water consumed.

Another common misconception is that water charges form part of business rates and often new businesses move into premises and do not realise they need to pay for water. After a time, sometimes a couple of years, they will get a bill from Business Stream demanding payment including back payment. This can be a shock to both cash flow and the business owner. If this happens you are best to contact business stream (They act on behalf of Scottish Water) and try and arrange a payment plan incorporated into your, now, normal bills.
Www.business-stream.co.uk

In Scotland the way water bills are arrived at is not particularly fair. While most businesses have a water meter this accounts for a small proportion of the overall charges.

Water consumption is billed on the basis of metered supply. If you are not metered then it is based on your rateable value.

Waste or sewerage is based on 95% of metered water or 95% of the estimated consumption based on R.V.

There is a fixed charge element applied to all bills metered or un-metered this will depend on the size of your meter. There is a fixed charge for water in and a fixed charge for water out.

There will also be a drainage charge to cover flow of waste water from your property, including the roof, into the public drainage system.

For a full list of charges go to

http://www.business-stream.co.uk/sites/default/files/120820Fullchargingstatement12-13v4.pdf

Reassessment

This can apply only if you do not have a water meter and your water is calculated on the basis of your rateable value. The intention is to try and iron out the differences between businesses and the amount of water they might use. For instance a café and a bookshop will use differing amounts of water. In addition the number employees will have a bearing as will things like kitchen facilities and toilets.

This can be done by using the calculator on the business stream website.

Examples

A client with retail premises contacted me regarding extremely high water bills. They had a meter and to all intents and purposes were being charged the correct amounts by the meter readings.

I contacted the utility company and requested a check of bills as I felt that the water bill bore no relation to what was being carried out on the premises. My first thought was that there may be some kind of major leakage that was not being picked up. The answer turned out to be much simpler.

The meter was being shared with another business in premises directly behind the retail frontage. This was a commercial car wash business! New meters were fitted to each business and the client received a refund for the overpayments.

Another client, an accountant received a large water bill (£2,000) for his office which is a single office sub-let in a large building. On contacting the water company I suggested that they were billing the accountant for the entire building. This was, in fact, the case and it was agreed that the landlord/owner of the building should be contacted to ascertain who the renters of the various offices were. The most common solution to this is that the owner of the building is responsible and they sub charge their clients for a fair proportion of the total bill. This will usually be agreed as part of the ongoing rent within the overall lease.

A small business who had been in situ for a number of years was given the opportunity to expand within the existing premises as they were being reconfigured. All appeared to be well until they became aware of a new set of invoices with a new account number from the water supplier. After questioning this it became clear that this was for a water meter that should have been removed with the reconfiguration. Despite being assured on numerous occasions that this would be resolved a monthly direct debit continued to be removed from the businesses bank account. When I became involved we were in our sixth year of trying to resolve the situation. I immediately got in touch with my contact at the utility company. This resulted in an engineer being dispatched to the premises and the problem being resolved in a matter of days. The client received a refund of nearly £4,000. A good example of getting professional help, bearing in mind that it had taken six years and a small forest worth of paper not to mention endless phone calls to get absolutely nowhere.

Road Closures – When a road is to be closed the local authority are obliged to let those affected know when it will happen and the projected length of time you will be affected. Most closures will be short in duration and cause minimal disruption.

In the instances where it is clear that it will cause the businesses a problem you should sit down with the council and try and mitigate the effects. Things such as extra signs showing that the businesses are accessible and open. The provision of a pedestrian access to the businesses.

In cases where this is likely to be a long term problem or it over runs, considerably, the anticipated time you may be able to claim compensation and get a reduction in your rates bill.

To claim any compensation you will have to demonstrate that you have been adversely affected by the problem

This will, normally, be done by comparing like for like figures with previous trading periods.

When you are seeking a rates rebate this again will need to be shown clearly why you are claiming. You will need to show a material change in your circumstances. This is a little harder to do and you should seek advice.

Disputes about work by Local Councils or utilities damaging your business.

The law allows for the utility companies and local authorities to carry out remedial work. Local businesses should be informed in writing in ample time of the proposed work and consulted about how best to mitigate the effects.

You should be given a clear idea of how long the disruption will last and what, if anything, they will be doing to mitigate this disruption. Things like newspaper adverts or additional signage directing customers to access points and letting them know that the businesses are still operating.

What happens if the work over-runs? This is not an unusual occurrence and the effects can range from irksome to devastating. If the work is either major and is scheduled to last a long time or has overrun badly there are several remedies open to you. The most likely one is to claim against the contractor for loss of business caused by the workings. This will require proof, usually a direct comparison of a comparable periods trading as against those figures for the duration of the problem. Another, but more difficult to access, way is to ask for a rates reduction for the period based on a material change of circumstances. For either of the suggested remedies I would suggest using a third party with experience of dealing with this type of problems.

Example

A hairdresser in a coastal town was badly affected by road closures and parking restrictions during a visit by the Tall Ships Race. The council argued that the closures and restrictions were for security reasons and were therefore unavoidable.

The client had only been in business for 9 months and had no comparable figures for the same period the year before. As the event was over a weekend they were able to show that compared to "normal" weekends the takings were reduced by around 50%.

In the end the local authority refused to compensate on the basis that it would set a precedent and limit their power to take this type of decision.

A cycle shop in a town centre complex was suffering a downturn because road works were blocking access to the part of the centre that the business was in. The contractors had put up "business as usual" signs along with directional arrows. A sign for the shop was not allowed as it would require planning permission according to the local authority.

The works were due to take 6 weeks but had seriously over run and were approaching 4 months and Christmas was on the way, a very busy time for a cycle shop.

After discussions with the council an exterior sign was allowed which did help with business. In the longer term the client made a claim for lost business and also a rebate on their business rates. They were able to clearly show a loss in takings over the comparable previous periods going back five years and because of the overrun they proved a material change to the business circumstances. The business was given the rebate and the contractor compensated them for the period beyond the original estimated time for the works of 6 weeks

Local Bureaucracy

How does this differ from the previous section covering disputes with local councils? The following are examples of how local bureaucracy can impinge on your business and how difficult it is to counteract.

Local Authorities will often make pronouncements or bring in local bye laws which on the face of it seem fair enough. They then fail to realise the impact this can have on local businesses.

An excellent example of this is a situation that I know exists in at least two council areas in Central Scotland. There was a decision to ban "A" advertising boards on the pavements as they were considered to be a hazard to pedestrians.

Quite right you might think people need clear access. The problem was that in both instances they were historical town centres and had a number of alleys off the high street where many small businesses were housed. They relied on the "A" boards to direct prospective customers to their premises.

Even after arranging meetings between local business groups and the council they refused to budge. I even went as far as to suggest a solution based on what happens in New York. They have a local ordinance that allows one "A" board per business but it must be chained and it cannot be more than one metre from the building line. To me this was a positive solution which addressed the concerns of both parties. However "local bureaucracy" prevailed.

Often you will find yourself the victim of totally illogical decisions. For example a fast food vendor with all the requisite licenses and an excellent reputation for food quality and cleanliness was informed, with no prior notification, that with immediate effect he would have to set up no closer than 250 yards from the local high school. Initially this was to be on a trial basis.

Of course it is understandable that local education departments are keen to ensure that the pupils, in the main, eat healthily and they felt that by doing this they were encouraging this.

The only problem was that within this arbitrary 250 yards exclusion zone for fast food vans, there a café, a Chinese restaurant and a fish and chip shop all selling fast food to the high school pupils.

When questioned about this the councils argument was that they had no control over the retail premises but could control fast food purveyors via the licensing system. I argued that surely the responsibility lay with the school and they should tackle the problem of pupils leaving school premises rather than punish local small businesses.

What this example does illustrate is that your business will be open to these kind of vagaries and you should, where possible, be aware of the local councils thinking on local businesses. Early warning is the key, get to know the local councilor and hopefully he will alert you to any changes that will affect you.

Debt Disputes

If you are in dispute over a debt you owe ensure that you write to the creditor and clearly state why you are questioning the account and keep a copy. If the creditor decides to proceed to collection and the Sheriff Officers or Bailiffs attend your premises to poind goods you can, at least show them why you are not paying. This is only valid if the enforcement is being carried out on the creditor's behalf without a court order

Before things reach this stage you will have had plenty of warning. Lawyers letters, court summons and finally, if you do nothing, an order from the court that the outstanding sum be collected.

Court is where the disputed claim can be defended by you. If the court does not agree it will order you to pay. It will then proceed to enforcement.

If you do owe the money and are having problems paying it try and reach an agreement with the creditor to pay it in instalments. From their point of view this is a better solution than, perhaps, getting nothing

If you are faced by Sheriff Officers or Bailiffs try and get them to agree to take some payment. This will result in the debt being reduced and the preceding paper work will have to be reworked as the amount of the date will have changed. This will buy you time only.

Bad Debts and Debt Collection

As a small business this is often a situation that many find difficult to know how best to approach the problem. There will be larger customers who will, no matter what terms you state on your contract or invoice, take their time to pay. Your decision at this point is to decide is it worth your while waiting for payment? You are effectively assisting their cash flow to your detriment. It may be that they give you a considerable amount of work and it is best to keep them onside as you cannot afford to lose their business.

This is a solution up to a point if they are consistent and prolonged late payers you must look at how much the cash flow shortage is costing your business by way of overdraft charges if this applies. This is a basic calculation you must carry out if you are running a business overdraft. If the result is that your profit margin that pays your wages and all overheads is reduced or compromised you have a decision to make.

There are a number of ways to approach poor payers. In the first instance a gentle reminder of your payment terms with a copy of the invoice. At this point put a deadline date of when you expect payment to be made. This will depend on how far overdue they are. If they have only recently become overdue anything between 5 and 10 working days is not unreasonable.

Keep a close eye on the account to ensure payment has been made. If the debt continues to be outstanding the next move will be a debt collection letter. In my experience the standard letters are ineffective, I always try and personalise mine. I have produced a sample of such a letter.

Sample Letter

*Dear *********,*

Reference Outstanding Invoice

I am disappointed that I find myself having to contact you again regarding the outstanding invoice. I feel that after I have carried out the work as per your instructions and with our ongoing dialogue throughout the process that an element of trust existed.

Having attempted to discover if there was some reason for your failure to pay I have not had the courtesy of any reply. In my business respect is a vital part of how I work. I respect my clients and their privacy and as a consequence expect that respect to be returned. I am prepared to allow you one final opportunity to transfer the funds as requested, to be in our account within 5 working days. Please see statement below.

Despite several attempts and your promise to pay, payment of your account has still not been received. If full payment is not received by [date] court action will be taken against you. If you allow this to happen you will incur court costs and you may forfeit your credit status because your name will be recorded by the major credit reference agencies. This may deter others from supplying you.

You are also being charged debt recovery costs and statutory interest of 8% above the reference rate (fixed for the six month period within which date the invoices became overdue) pursuant to the late payment legislation. To stop this from happening please pay in full now or contact me to put forward your proposals.

Yours sincerely

There are a number of ways of dealing with this problem. You can outsource the collection to a third party, probably not cost effective but this will depend on the size of the debt. Invoice factoring, where you can assign the invoiced debt in exchange for around 80% of the invoice value. The company to whom you have assigned the invoice will then let the customer no that this happened and that the funds should be paid to them. Once they are in receipt of the final settlement you receive the 20% balance less the agreed charges for using the service The benefit of this method is that you get the majority of your money immediately which will be beneficial to your cash flow. You also have your credit control function carried out by a third party, relieving you of the pressure of ensuring payments. There is a drawback in as much as you may have to put in place a personal guarantee. This will depend on the size of your company and the type of clients that you work with.

Another radical solution which is possible whether you are the debtor or the creditor. If you are the debtor and owe a supplier for goods you buy regularly it may be possible to convince them to continue to supply you on the basis that you will pay up front by bank transfer. This will include a percentage surcharge that will be used to reduce your outstanding debt.

This is a risk for both sides and tends to only work in certain situations. For instance if you are a manufacturer and buy parts from a supplier without which you cannot carry on in business the supplier can either go to court to get settlement the end result of which could be the business going bust. The downsides for the supplier are that a business in administration/liquidation may eventually have no money or not enough to pay the debt.

The costs of going to court add to the debt and the court process can be lengthy.

From the creditors viewpoint the same arguments apply and you have to make the decision based on your knowledge and what is best for you.

The Unexpected

There will be things that happen that you will not have anticipated, problems you couldn't foresee. I have dealt with members problems and acted as a confidential buffer and trouble-shooter dealing with every issue under the sun. I deal on an almost daily basis with businesses having problems with their bank, with customers, with suppliers, councils, utility companies and government.

In addition to the more normal issues and problems there are things that will appear from left field that require attention. The following examples are extreme but they do show that there is always something you didn't allow for budget for.

The Dead Cat

The client a vet contacted me. They had, the day before taken into care a cat only to discover it was seriously and terminally ill. They asked that the animal be left overnight as they wanted to do some tests and keep an eye on the animal overnight.

Unfortunately the cat succumbed during the night. The following mid-morning the owner phoned the vet to discover the cat had sadly died. To add to their grief they were then told that the body of the cat had been dispatched that morning to a company in the North East of England to be cremated. They were distraught as they had intended to bury the cat in their own garden.

I spoke with the vet and also the pet cremation company to try and resolve the situation. Due to regulations and health and safety they could not return the remains. I brokered a deal where the ashes of the pet would be returned for burial. Not the ideal solution but it did, partially, resolve the issue for the client.

I have included this rather curious case as an example of where, in this case, a clear agreement between the vet and the owner would have stopped this happening in the first place.

The Dead Horse

Don't ask! I seem to attract this kind of case. The owner of the horse, a local farmer, had been visited by his vet as he had a horse with some problems. Part of the consultation involved an internal exam by the vet. This I will leave to your imagination, think drug mules and rubber gloves.

Shortly after the vet left the horse began to bleed profusely from its rear end. The farmer contacted the local vet hospital who he knew had a specialist equestrian section. The horse was taken to the hospital, sedated and unfortunately died. The farmer was asked if it was ok to cremate the animal, he agreed.

He then contacted the vet to make a claim on his insurance. The vet however proceeded to deny that his examination had caused the internal bleed. As the body had been cremated there was no definitive proof as to the cause.

I became involved and spoke to all parties. As the body had been cremated there was no way to prove this was the cause. The end result was that the hospital gave evidence that the bleeding was likely to have at least was due in part to the internal exam. In the end the insurance did pay out albeit a reduced amount for the loss of the animal.

Again, if there is any doubt in the outcome ensure you keep a solid evidence trail. This applies to lots of situations not just the extreme example here.

Bull Sperm

This is a bizarre problem that only became a problem because of procedures that were not clear. The client's business was a specialist in artificial insemination of cattle. He had collected a considerable amount of bull sperm that day, around £15,000 worth. He then took back to his own premises for temporary storage before taking it to be frozen for later use.

It was at this point that, following a few days of Foot and Mouth alerts that an Animal Movement Order was issued. Our client was informed that the order applied to his flask. If he could not get it transferred to the freezing facility he would lose the contents.

I investigated the situation and sought expert opinion. The general advice was that the Department of Agricultural and Fisheries were wrong and there was no reason for the flask not to be moved. I arranged a meeting with a local department employee and discovered that the situation was not something specifically covered by the regulations. After a series of intense calls and meetings they were convinced that the order did not apply.

I have included this rather bizarre episode to illustrate that just because a Government department is involved it is not necessarily correct in its application of the rules. Always challenge the status quo.

I have learned that the old adage "a problem shared is a problem halved" most times rings true.

If you need assistance ask for it. Whether it is via friends and family who may have the experience and knowledge you need. Perhaps through being a member of a trade organisation. Or, by hiring someone like me, an experienced and successful trouble shooter and mentor, in the long term it will often pay off.

Most importantly do not put problems to one side, try and deal with them right away. If you need help ask for it in plenty of time. It is no use looking for assistance once the problem has passed a certain point. Sheriff's Officers or Bailiffs are a good example of when it is too late

Chapter 12

Collaboration

While the title of this guide is "The Loneliness of a Small Business Owner" there are ways to mitigate that isolation.

A relatively easy way of both combating that "loneliness" and expanding the relative range of services you can offer. It will also allow you to tender for some public service contracts where alone you would be too small but as a group you would be able to bid and provide the services required.

In an uncertain economy it makes sense for small businesses to collaborate allowing them to extend their reach into new and broader markets. New technology and communication systems are making it much simpler for businesses to co-operate even if they are some distance apart. Used properly this technology allows the smooth delivery of a range of services from various locations.

It is a means of offering a range of services in addition to your own but as a single package. You can share each other's client lists assuming the services offered are not similar and are complimentary to your own this can be beneficial to both parties.

How do you go about starting a collaborative relationship?

Start by deciding if you want only to work with people in the same field as you are operating or could you partner other services which are complimentary to your own. If you are a Management

Consultant you may wish to consider HR Consultants as partners to increase the scope of possible customers.

Do you want to limit your collaboration to others in your own area or do want to spread your wings and widen your horizons by looking farther afield?

To start the process of forming a partnership personal experience leads me to believe that forming a data base of likely targets and writing a standard letter start with who you are and what you do followed by a list of logical reasons of why it would be mutually beneficial for you to work together. It may be you have a specific project in mind or you feel that being able to offer complimentary services would be a good way forward for you both.

This should be followed by a face to face meeting with the prospective partners where all aspects of any agreement should be thrashed out. It may be that you only wish to have a mutual referral system with links on each other's web sites if so a handshake and verbal agreement will suffice. However, should you be planning to work together on a specific contract or project, or bidding on a joint tender then a written agreement laying out how everything works and how it impinges on each partner business should be drawn up and signed by all parties involved. It should include the division of responsibilities, basically who does what, and also how budgets are funded and earnings distributed.

You may for instance want to agree on how much you would want to spend on marketing the service or product and how the cost of this should be met by each partner business. If you are planning a bid for contact work this can often mean a great deal of research and pre bid work. You must decide before you start how his work is to be paid for.

If one of the partners has expertise perhaps the agreement would be that his staff carry out the work and the other partners are billed an agreed portion of the cost.

You can collaborate with a range of other services on a fixed period basis, on and open ended basis or form partnerships for specific projects or tenders. Whatever the reason or basis for working together, you should always carefully research who you are going to be working with. Hence a face to face meeting is best. How long of they been in business, what is their personal

The previous chapter on collaboration shows ways of adapting and adding to your services. It also gives you other avenues for professional advice and expertise.

Running a small business can be lonely, however, if you ensure you have your partner, family and friends onside and they understand what it is you are doing this support can be invaluable.

Join a trade organisation, your local Chamber of Commerce or the Federation of Small Businesses can be ideal choices. The Chamber will give you a great many networking opportunities. While the FSB offer an excellent range of advice, help-lines and benefits.

Consider mentoring, never be afraid to ask for advice whatever problem you may have you can be pretty sure someone else has already had and resolved something similar.

I hope I have succeeded and that whatever stage you are in your business life you have found something useful in the guide.

Disclaimer

All information related to various Government and non - Government agencies including web addresses and available services is correct at time of going to press. You should always confirm that there have been no changes to said services and web addresses in the intervening period.

www.ingramcontent.com/pod-product-compliance
Lightning Source LLC
Chambersburg PA
CBHW072210170526
45158CB00002BA/534